Giovanni della Casa's Poem Book
Ioannis Casae Carminum Liber

FLORENCE 1564

MEDIEVAL & RENAISSANCE
TEXTS & STUDIES

VOLUME 194

NEO-LATIN TEXTS AND TRANSLATIONS
Volume 1

Giovanni della Casa's Poem Book
Ioannis Casae Carminum Liber

FLORENCE 1564

Edited & Translated into Verse
with Commentary by
John B. Van Sickle

Arizona Center for Medieval and Renaissance Studies
Tempe, Arizona
1999

The photograph that appears on page vii is reprinted courtesy of Alinari/Art Resource, New York.

© Copyright 1999

Arizona Board of Regents for Arizona State University

Library of Congress Cataloging-in-Publication Data

Della Casa, Giovanni, 1503–1556.
   [Poems. English & Latin. Selections]
   Giovanni Della Casa's poem book = Ioannis [i.e. Jonnis] Casae carminum liber / edited & translated into verse with commentary by John B. Van Sickle.
      p. cm. — (Medieval & Renaissance Texts & Studies ; v. 194)
   ISBN 0-86698-236-1 (alk. paper)
   1. Della Case, Giovanni, 1503–1556—Translations into English. 2. Pastoral poetry, Latin (Medieval and modern)—Italy—Translations into English. 3. City and town life—Italy—Poetry. 4. Country life—Italy—Poetry. I. Van Sickle, John. II. Title. III. Title: Ioannis Casae carminum liber. IV. Title: Jonnis Casae carminum liber. V. Series: Medieval & Renaissance Texts & Studies (Series) ; v. 194.
PA8485.D636A28 1999
871'.04–dc21   99-19158
                                                                                                                  CIP

∞
This book is made to last.
It is set in Garamond,
smythe-sewn and printed on acid-free paper
to library specifications.

Printed in the United States of America

CONTENTS

Preface   ix

Introduction
    I   The Literary Fate   1
    II   The Life in Letters and Poems   5
    III   The System and Poetics of the Book   28
    IV   The History of the Edition   31

The Poem Book
    I   A Country Cure for the Sick City   40
    II   The City Blamed for Sickness in the Poet   42
    III   The Healthy Style of Poetic Life   44
    IV   The City Women Blamed   50
    V   To Flee the City for a Cure   52
    VI   Honoring a Florentine Master's Gifts   54
    VII   Warning against Sly Flattery   58
    VIII   Warning against Shifty Fortune   60
    IX   Praising the Healer of the West   62
    X   A Brief for Brevity in the Book   68
    XI   Honoring a Princess, Blaming Himself   68
    XII   Consoling a Princess, Praising a Hero   70
    XIII   Praising a Florentine Master's Gifts   74
    XIV-VI   No Cure for a Country Ill   76

Commentary and Notes   79

Appendices
    I   Punctuation Sampler   117
    II   Selected Letters   119

Bibliography   147

Index   151

Pope Paul III (Alessandro Farnese) with his grandsons Cardinal Alessandro (the patron and intimate of Casa) and Ottavio Farnese (who after 1547 abetted by his brother defied his grandfather to keep the dukedom of Parma): portrayed by Titian in 1545, when Casa also sat for his portrait while serving as Pope Paul's nuncio to Venice.
Museo Nazionale de Capodimonte, Naples, Italy.

PREFACE

Evidence that Giovanni della Casa composed a poetic sequence in the tradition of Virgil and Horace first attracted me to him. Only later did I learn of "the hot debate over the character of early modern Italian culture" and realize that my study also served the need for "More works detailing the contradictions and inconsistencies of persons in this era—especially churchmen" in order to create "the detailed, human and carefully nuanced landscape truly worthy of describing Tridentine Italy."[1] Since the *Poem Book* has never been studied or translated and was last reprinted nearly three hundred years ago, I provide an edition and the first translation into any language. Each poem also receives a brief commentary, which outlines themes, sketches the dramatic situation, provides basic information about persons, circumstances, and traditions both mythological and literary, and suggests ways in which the piece fits into the sequence.

Casa's own "inconsistencies and contradictions" unfold amidst intrigues involving the papal and Florentine courts, the Venetian aristocracy, the ruthless Farnese clan and the French royal house. The poet assumes by turns the voices of the orator and moralist, moving between vituperation and praise, between pithy example and eloquent flight, between earnest counsel and learned play—lively voices that I have sought to make actual in the translation. Through it all, he also devotes himself to shaping a narrative, justifying an ethical and aesthetic stance, and rounding out his oeuvre. For ideas on how he can coordinate diverse pieces to unitary ends in a poetic sequence, he looks to the classical exemplars of Propertius, Catullus, and Horace. How original he was

---

[1] William V. Hudon, review of Elisabeth G. Gleason, *Gasparo Contarini: Venice, Rome and Reform* (Berkeley: University of California Press, 1993), in *Renaissance Quarterly* 48 (1995): 624.

in adapting them has escaped notice and might well have continued to do so, without the recent growth in understanding of poetic sequences, including my own work on Virgil's *Book of Bucolics*.[2] As a close rereading of Horatian sequences, Casa's achievement has no peer. Its nuanced unity furnishes a new touchstone by which to test the principles of coherence in every putative *liber* or *canzoniere* from Petrarch onwards; indeed the rediscovery of such a work in Latin fills out the portrait of its author as a humanist in the Petrarchan vein, producing verse ensembles in both Italian and Latin, even as the Renaissance came to its bitter close.

My search for Casa's manuscripts was facilitated by a PSC-CUNY Faculty Research Award. I was fortunate to benefit from the legendary learning and generosity of P. O. Kristeller, who remembered where the material was, told me how to get there, and urged me not to give up. The librarians I found at the ends of the search were unstintingly helpful: at the Munich Staatsbibliothek, Biblioteca Marciana, Bibliothèque Nationale, British Library, and the Folger Shakespeare Library, where I was aided by Werner Gundersheimer and his staff. At the Biblioteca Apostolica Vaticana it was a special joy to work in the climate fostered by Father Leonard Boyle and to benefit from the expert and unstinting instruction of Carlo Buonocuore. For counsel and gifts of their scholarly work, I am grateful to Guido Baldassari, Teodolinda Barolini, Eduardo Saccone, Claudio Scarpati, and Fred Nichols. The referees of the press were very acute and helpful, more generous of learning and care than one has any right to expect. At the climactic moment, Robert Bjork supervened with bold editorial vision and William Gentrup brought priceless acumen and patience to getting details right. Such flaws as remain are my own.

At various stages, I presented some of my results at the Renaissance Society of America, Renaissance Seminar of Columbia University, Brown University Classics Department, and Philological Seminar of Professor Scevola Mariotti in Rome, receiving many helpful suggestions. I carried out the translation while a guest of the Rockefeller Foundation at Villa Serbelloni (Bellagio, Lake Como) under circumstances uniquely calculated to sustain and inspire, recalling Casa's own retreat at the abbey of Narvesa. Help in finding the abbey, now a ruin of war, came from Emilio Pianezzola, who led our trek late one March afternoon across the plain from

---

[2] Conveniently summarized in John B. Van Sickle, "Staging Vergil's Future and Past," *Classical Journal* 93 (1997): 216, note 3. Cf. also the Bucolics section of my webpage, http://academic.brooklyn.cuny.edu/classics/jvsickle.

Padua, where Casa met Bembo and spent some of his happiest years. To my wife, Gail Levin, who encouraged me when the road seemed very long, I am happy to dedicate the result.

July 1998
Stone Sets, East Hampton
jvsickle@brooklyn.cuny.edu

INTRODUCTION

I. The Literary Fate

Painfully debilitated by illness, dying under a strange roof, disappointed in all he had tried, Giovanni della Casa (1503–1556) was so anxious about his reputation as a writer that he ordered his works destroyed. Measured by the ideal of literary humanism that came to the Renaissance from Petrarch (1304–1374),[1] Casa had gone astray. As a young man, wealthy and intelligent, channeled into legal studies, like Petrarch he had turned to poetry, winning aristocratic and humanist friends, except that Casa had a penchant for verse that was wickedly obscene.[2] Soon, again like Petrarch, Casa found powerful patronage: the brilliant, cultivated, and worldly young Alessandro Cardinal Farnese (1519–1589). Farnese was created cardinal in 1534, aged only 14, when his grandfather and namesake became pope as Paul III.[3] Patronage brought opportunity for preferment in the church, which Petrarch had declined, but Casa took. He entered ecclesiastical administration, rose to the rank of monsignor, then archbishop, and was sent in 1544 as papal nuncio to Venice. He aspired to a cardinal's hat himself.

The new envoy came well introduced by the long-time friend he left to enjoy his Rome apartment as a guest. The noble Venetian Pietro Bembo (1470–1547) had turned from the worldly pursuits of his forebears to devote himself to classical learning. He created a studied style in prose and verse, both Latin and Italian, in Petrarch's steps.[4] While ensconced in Casa's exquisitely appointed lodging, Bembo managed also

---

[1] *Rime* 60, "Errai gran tempo," cited by Eduardo Saccone, *Le buone e le cattive maniere: Letteratura e Galateo nel cinquecento*. Ricerca (Bologna: Il Mulino, 1992), 126–28.

[2] Antonio Santosuosso, "Inediti casiani con appunti sulla vita, il pensiero e le opere dello scrittore fiorentino," *La rassegna della letteratura italiana* 79 (1975): 461–95; Antonio Santosuosso, *Vita di Giovanni Della Casa* (Roma: Bulzoni, 1979), 40–51.

[3] Alessandro Farnese (1468–1549).

[4] Saccone, *Le buone e le cattive maniere*, 119–25.

to obtain the cardinalate from Paul III: it seemed a favorable augury for his host.

There were objections. The nuncio fathered a Venetian bastard, compounding his youthful notoriety. To be sure, this pope had fathered four children and elevated Bembo, who had three. But they represented the secular Renaissance, which was yielding to more stringent spirituality under pressures from the reformist North. Casa had been born too late.

Other objections came from his native Florence. Exiled opponents of the Medici regime frequented him in Venice. Though not openly in opposition, Casa publicly and repeatedly praised Venice for preserving its traditional republican freedoms. The implied nostalgia for a freer Florence fueled Medici distrust.

The death of Pope Paul in 1549 ended Casa's curial hopes. Back in Rome, ill and tormented, he denounced ambition and sought a different way of life. One option was the reformed spirituality practiced by many of his friends: embracing pastoral duty, shepherding the archbishopric he had yet to see. The pastoral he chose, instead, was Petrarchan: returning to Venice in 1551, he retired to the countryside to write.

Petrarch had rejected the papal court for his villa in the Vaucluse, giving literary and philosophical withdrawal new currency.[5] Valuing the country as a restorative morally superior to the city, Petrarch inspired the Renaissance emulation of a pattern of high culture in Greece and Rome. Although a plebeian Socrates might scorn trees and prefer the bustling public square, privileged Plato withdrew to a grove and Epicurus to a garden. The very word for leisure became a term for study, "school." Cicero and his aristocratic friends would withdraw to villas overlooking Rome from nearby heights. There Cicero retreated, when political life became too perilous, to compose dialogues, which portrayed philosophical and literary conversations in the same rural settings but at a remove in time. Likewise Horace rooted his poetic imagination in the country, although his was a less conspicuous villa behind more distant hills, more in keeping with his lower political profile and moderate creed.

The Petrarchan ideal had never been enough for Casa and in practice it soon palled. He kept in touch with his patron. When Cardinal Farnese won favor with a new pope (Paul IV, elevated in 1555), he placed Casa as papal secretary. Hopes of the purple revived, only to fall before

---

[5] David R. Coffin, "The Affluent Italian and His Country Residence," *The Villa in the Life of Renaissance Rome* (Princeton: Princeton University Press, 1979), 9–10

the old objections. Disillusioned and ever more painfully ill, Casa died the next year, still only "Monsignor."[6] This title, which he tried so hard to put behind, still identifies him in the Italian schoolrooms and literary handbooks, even on a street sign in the Venetian countryside where he retired to write.

"Monsignor della Casa" would not enjoy even his present modicum of fame were it not for what he wrote during his brief retreat and back in Rome on his deathbed ordered burned. He expressed his wish to his sister's son, Annibale Rucellai (?–1601), whom he had educated like a child of his own. But anyone so well imbued with classical culture would detect in the despairing gesture the shadow of Rome's most famous poet. Legend had it that the dying Virgil ordered his unfinished epic destroyed, but that Augustus had the *Aeneid* published, to the greater glory of both emperor and poet.

Rucellai facilitated publication. He housed for two months in Venice a life-long friend of his uncle's, Carlo Gualteruzzi, who edited and saw through the press the Italian works in 1558, just two years after Casa's death. Among them, the ironical treatise on manners known as *Galateo*, emulating the prose style of Boccaccio, won immediate popularity throughout Europe. Translated into Latin, Spanish, French, German and several times into English, it became a by-word. Its model of behavior still seemed marketable as late as 1811 to an enterprising printer in Baltimore, Maryland.[7] Promoting sales, he pirated a London version and combined it with a handbook on carving meats at table. With that Casa vanished from the English-speaking market, absorbed and obliterated by newer arbiters and modes, though aspiring cultural arbiters and sycophants in any century might profit still.

The 1558 volume also included Casa's sequence of Italian lyric poems, which have received praise from poets, beginning with Tasso, and from critics:

> All of Della Casa's poems express a fundamental anxiety and an inquietude about love or ambition which are often coupled with a longing for release, peace, and even death. The combination of this

---

[6] Cf. the discussion of mannerist culture by Antonio Sole, *Cognizione del Reale e Letteratura in Giovanni Della Casa* (Roma: Bulzoni, 1981), 11–12, with notes and bibliographical references. For the complex and contradictory forces in Casa's own personality, see Saccone, *Le buone e le cattive maniere*, 148–50.

[7] *Galateo; or, A Treatise on politeness and delicacy of manners: from the Italian of Monsignor Giovanni de la Casa . . . also The honours of the Table, with the whole art of carving illustrated with a variety of cuts* (Baltimore: printed for George Hill; B. Edes, printer, 1811).

troubled content and the sublime style made Della Casa's fewer than eighty lyrics among the best of the sixteenth century.[8]

Readers of the *Rime* have sensed the clash of polished Petrarchan manner with harsh disillusionment in love, in curial ambition, and in literary endeavor. The lyrics document the hold of Petrarch's cultural ideal and its fracture under historical and personal stress.

The success of Casa's works in Italian replicates the literary fate of Petrarch and Boccaccio in an earlier age:

> The glory of the Italian communes was a thing of the past, and it was inevitable that in a society increasingly dominated by princely courts Petrarch's effort to create a secular role for the man of letters should be aristocratic in orientation. After 1350 both Petrarch and Boccaccio threw the weight of their influence on the side of aristocratic culture in Latin; their audience was learned and international, not peninsular, let alone municipal. But both are beloved for the other side of their genius and for their writings in Italian.[9]

Casa, too, wrote Latin for an aristocratic culture, and these works that pleased his princely patron and a select, international audience enjoy today much less than the limited reputation accorded Petrarch's. Even their debut was halting. Not until 1564, eight years after Casa's death, did there appear a slim volume entitled *Latina monimenta Ioannis Casae* (Latin Monuments of Giovanni della Casa).

For the Latin, Casa's nephew found an appropriate editor, more scholarly and patrician than Gualteruzzi, in a Florentine friend of his uncle, Pier Vettori (1499–1585). The aristocratic orientation of the project was clear. On June 10, 1564, Vettori sent the volume to Casa's old patron, whom Vettori had long courted himself,[10] assuring the cardinal that the book honored the Farnese family. Interest proved strong enough that the publisher issued a second edition (1567), but

---

[8] Wayne Rebhorn. "Della Casa, Giovanni," in *Dictionary of Italian Literature* (Westport, 1979), 166; cf. the full discussion in Sole, *Cognizione*, 8–13; Klaus Ley, "Die 'scienza civile' des Giovanni della Casa," *Litteratur als Gesellschaftskunst in der Gegenreformation* (Winter, 1984): 196–98.

[9] Robert M. Durling, ed. and trans., *Petrarch's Lyric Poems: The* Rime Sparse *and Other Lyrics* (Cambridge: Harvard, 1976), 4.

[10] Vettori to Cardinal Farnese, Florence, 10 June 1564; cited by Antonio Santosuosso, "Le opere italiane del Casa e l'edizione principe di quelle latine nei carteggi vettoriani del British Museum," *La Bibliofilia* 79 (1977): 63. Cf. Appendix II, 1564.vi.10.

nothing motivated further reprints in Italy, neither Farnese nor Venetian themes. The Latin texts do appear in the compendious editions of Casa produced in the *settecento*, but these of course were predicated on the continued fame of his Italian works.

Even farther from their original aristocratic and ecclesiastical matrix, the Latin poems with some translations from Greek were extracted by a northern German disciple of Vettori's for teaching Latin style in schools (Helmstedt, 1610).[11] Once more for German pupils the entire volume was reprinted a century later (Magdeburg, 1709).[12] Some treatises, such as Casa's life of Bembo, have drawn the attention of recent scholars,[13] but not the *Carminum Liber*, although Vettori gave it pride of place at the volume's head. Yet the *Poem Book* sheds unexpected light on the conflicted passions and ideals that motivated Casa's retreat and its literary output, breaking new ground in the sequence tradition inherited from Petrarch and classical Rome.

II. *The Life in Letters and Poems*

The restless retreat was only the last and most drastic reversal documented in poems and letters that Casa exchanged through much of his life. He and his friends modeled themselves on the Roman letter writers Cicero and Pliny and their humanist emulators from Petrarch on.[14] Such precedents conferred a literary aura on the obligatory communications between men who found their livelihood in scattered bishoprics and courts.

As early as 1510, when the boy was only seven years old, Casa's banker father bought his second son a canonship. Religion would not be one of his passions.[15] Growing up in Rome, Casa went to study law at Bologna. Never finishing, he did make fast friends before moving to the university at Padua in Venetian territory where he encountered Bembo.

---

[11] *Ioan. Casae Carmina et Orationes Plœrœque Thucydidis in Latinum Sermonem Ab Eodem Conversae*, ed. Johannes Casellius (Helmstadt: In Acad. Iulia Excudebat Iacobvs Lvcivs, 1610).

[12] *Ioannis Casae Latina Monimenta*, ed. Nicolaus Hieronymus Gundlingius (Magdeburg: Officina Libraria Rengeriana, 1709).

[13] Sole, *Cognizione*, 14–15; Saccone, *Le buone e le cattive maniere*, 120, cites an 1852 translation into Italian of Casa's life of Bembo.

[14] Petrarch discovered the manuscript of Cicero's *Letters to Atticus* in 1345 and made them the models for his own letters: Durling, *Petrarch's Lyric*, 2.

[15] Santosuosso, *Vita*, 20ff.

From the start, wealth and wit let Casa form the network of acquaintances that would flourish throughout his life. He could indulge, too, in the old aristocratic alternation of country with city life, since his family owned property at Mugello outside Florence. From there, in the summer of 1525, he writes to Lodovico Beccadelli, a noble Bolognese and lifelong friend,[16] returning a sonnet by Francisco Maria Molza (1489–1544) and begging one by Beccadelli himself. To their mutual friend Gualteruzzi, his later editor, he praises a sonnet and a "divine" letter from that "divine" talent Bembo. He exhorts Gualteruzzi not to pay him back a loan but keep the money for some need, perhaps to publish a book. Money and publishing would be recurrent themes. Two years later (1527) it was with Beccadelli that Casa withdrew to the country to peruse Cicero for seventeen months in pastoral calm while imperial troops pillaged Rome.[17]

Back in Rome by 1532, Casa continued to frequent literary circles, in particular the new academies then forming as independent intellectual centers. Typical of that life was a man like Molza, who abandoned a wife and children in Modena, attached himself as a poet-courtier to Ippolito Cardinal Dei Medici and, when Ippolito was poisoned in 1535, found a new protector in Casa's patron. Molza flattered the cardinal in facile elegies that play on the ideal of rural retreat. He imagines escape from Rome's heat in summer to cool havens, where the cardinal would have the guidance of the goddess Pallas to read Tibullus, Virgil, and Horace. There the grandfather (Paul III) would enjoy the company of his cardinal grandson, whom Molza hails in heroic style as joyful Alexander "second hope of great Rome" (*magnae spes altera Romae*, quoting the flattery of Aeneas's son in Virgil's *Aeneid* 12.168).[18] This was the same Molza who affected the French custom of kissing women in public, as Casa complained, adding that "His beard will be plucked and perhaps something else."[19] Molza has been judged "a gay and dissolute spendthrift."[20] Not that the judgment is modern only. Molza was called a "gagliofacio" (roughly "beggar, ne'er-do-well, rascal") by his friend and

---

[16] Casa (Badia) to Beccadelli (Bologna or Pre d'Albino), July 1525, *Opere di Monsignor Giovanni della Casa*, vol. 4 (Milan: Società Tipografica de'Classici Italiani, 1806), 321–31.

[17] Santosuosso, *Vita*, 24–25.

[18] "Ad Alexandrum Farnesium Cardinalem," 35r–36r, and "In Paulum. III. Pont. Max." 38r–39v, in Johannes Paulus Ubaldinus, ed., *Carmina poetarum nobilium studio conquisita* (Milan: Antonius Antonianus, 1563).

[19] Casa (Florence) to Gualteruzzi (Rome), 1 January [1534], *Opere* (1806) 4:177.

[20] Alessandro Perosa and John Sparrow, *Renaissance Latin Verse: An Anthology* (London: Duckworth, 1979), 260.

Casa's Francesco Berni (1497?–1535): Berni himself became a byword for his obscene burlesque verse in Italian, *capitoli*, that epitomized cynical disaffection and impotent rage at the unbearable times.[21] It is indicative of Casa's values and attitudes that he could emulate Berni's rakish Italian and use Horatian Latin to praise Molza as a "wholesome heart washed by the healthful waters of the Pierian spring."[22]

Traits that contributed to Casa's last crisis appear already in a letter of 1532 from Rome to Beccadelli, who by then was serving as secretary to another mutual friend, Cosimo Geri (1512–1537), the youthful bishop of Fano, where Gualteruzzi had been born:

> You have seen something of the World, so, while we can, arrange to meet one day at Predalbino[23] to weep for our sins, with greater sweetness than we felt in committing them, though you perhaps do not have your conscience heavy as I do, nor would you allow me to speak thus in the plural.[24]

Five years have passed since they read Cicero in the country while Rome burned. Casa's "conscience" is "heavy"; yet his notion of how to lighten it is hardly Christian.

What weighed on Casa's conscience comes out in a letter to Beccadelli's superior, Geri (quotation marks indicate Latin citations in the original):

> ... I don't want Your Lordship to love me anymore so much from the heart, as you have done up to now, because I don't deserve it anymore, as I didn't deserve it even before: but now that I have put all judgment [*pensiero*] out in the cold [*in non cale*] and that a woman, "she indeed with her sweet lures," has changed me so much, I am unworthy that Your Lordship hold me so dear, as I know you do: if ever I return "to health," then you will love me: in this way "we will make vows and sternly choose a better attitude for ourselves," since I am lost and despair of human advice and help. ...[25]

---

[21] Santosuosso, "Inediti casiani," 461ff; idem, *Vita*, 40–51.
[22] See the present edition of *Carminium Liber* III.95; hereinafter cited as *CL*.
[23] Beccadelli's retreat in the country near Bologna: mentioned by Casa to Beccadelli, July 1525, *Opere* (1806) 4:325.
[24] 14 November 1532, *Opere* (1806) 4:339. See Appendix II for Italian texts.
[25] Casa (Rome) to Geri (Fano), 24 November 1532, *Opere* (1806) 4:341.

Confessing failure to live up to an ideal of male friendship, Casa speaks in terms that echo Petrarchan love, with Plato in the background.[26] His language becomes oblique: "put" lacks color, but *pensiero* has the color of its Latin origins (considering, weighing), as does *in non cale* (in not warm).[27] For the woman, he uses Latin: *dulcibus illa quidem illecebris* (she indeed with her sweet lures), which Virgil wrote of a cow that distracts and weakens bulls.[28] The rhetorical imbalance is enormous between the opaque self-image of nonchalance and the vivid evocation of aggressive female sexuality. Adding insult to injury, with "she changed me" Casa implies that by nature he was suited for ideal male friendship, if only he had not been spoiled by the female brute. Escalating his rhetoric, Casa draws on yet another familiar formula. "I am unworthy that Your Lordship . . ." echoes the confession and penitential disposition of the mass, *Domine, non sum dignus*. Finally, Casa paints himself as "lost," not unlike Dante's pilgrim as the *Commedia* begins.

Another appeal to Beccadelli and Geri comes two years later (1534). Casa evokes their "rule" to straighten out his life, which is bent beyond belief "back towards the Sirens of the World."[29] Again he casts himself in the role of victim, seduced by threatening female power—"Sirens," whose music kept sailors from reaching home. The theme of seduction by the Sirens' song recalls Homer's Odysseus, who stuffed with wax the ears of his companions so they would row on safely, but had himself bound to the mast so he could hear the fatal strains.

Casa found no such dodge. He indulged in prostitutes, contracted liver disease, wrote a satire in the style of Berni on the minuteness of his sexual organ.[30] He reveled in the world. Yet he complains of gossip in another letter to Geri (1535):[31] someone has spread rumors about his loves, making them out to be monstrous and inexplicable, while someone else has provoked curiosity about his verse in that censorious and

---

[26] On the ideological and psychological role of Petrarchism as escape from political turmoil, language of aristocracy, vehicle of emancipation from Latin, and obligatory rhetoric of love, when love is the essential form of *savoir faire*, see Santosuosso, *Vita*, 25.

[27] The expression derives from *calere* ("feel warmth, be warm": metaphorically "be in love with, zealous for, eager to" in Latin, then older Italian). The negation, which Casa uses, equating "cool" with "not caring," occurs also in Latin, Provençal, old French, and Spanish, surviving into modern French (and English) as *nonchalance*. See Ottorino Pianigiani, *Vocabolario etimologico della lingua italiana* (La Spezia: Melita, 1990), 213.

[28] Virgil, *Georgics* 3.217.

[29] Casa (Rome) to Beccadelli (Bologna), 7 August 1534, *Opere* (1806) 4:349.

[30] Santosuosso, *Vita*, 33–46.

[31] Casa (Rome) to Geri (Padua), 11 March 1535, *Opere* (1806) 4:350.

too spiritual divine, Alvise Priuli, who might better have been kept in the dark.

The verse in question was an epistle in Latin, which would eventually enter the *Carminum Liber*. By July Casa had still not sent it even to Geri, "Because I haven't been able to keep myself from being a bit obscure, and if I sent it written in my own hand, between the bad writing and the dark saying it would tire you out."[32] In a compliment to Geri for writing in Latin and doing it very well, he quotes Horace, "Just as, if I'm not mistaken, 'What more would a dear nurse desire for her sweet pupil, than to be wise and able to utter what he feels?.' "[33] As often, he uses a famous classical text to convey a particular emphasis: praise for Geri's Latin epistles by citing the classical master of epistles in verse. Casa goes on to promise a copy of his own epistle for Geri. But he insists it must not go outside their circle, in which affectionately he includes the poet Marc Antonio Flaminio (1498–1550), who was summering with Geri and Beccadelli in the country: "I wish him very happy nights, and many, since the hours in this season are so short." Flaminio belonged to Casa's literary coterie in Rome, including the "Academy of *Virtù*."[34]

In the epistle, Casa plays his favorite trick of deflecting blame to others. He grapples with the passions he so often confessed and never purged, once more calling on the help of traditional language: as a genre, the verse epistle had been turned by Horace into a measured and witty reflection on poetics and ethics. Its very use implied mastery of art and self. To embody the ideal, Casa picks Bembo. By idealizing him and defending him against detractors, portrayed as a vicious and carping crowd, Casa seeks to avert heat from his own life style. The audacity of making Bembo a cover might have been especially apparent to Geri, who was an intimate of both. Little wonder, too, if Casa wished to keep the poem from Bembo's fellow Venetian, the hypercritical and spiritual Priuli, who was unlikely to admire Bembo's erotic lyrics and the long relationship that produced three sons.

When Geri got the epistle, he queried not the ethics but details of style, to infer from Casa's response:

---

[32] Casa (Rome) to Geri (Bologna), 3 July 1535, *Opere* (1806) 4:352–53.

[33] Horace, *Epist.* 1.4.8–9: *quid voveat dulci nutricula maius alumno, quam sapere, et fari possit quae sentiat?*

[34] Santosuosso, *Vita*, 38.

The more experience you have with Horace's epistles, the less mine should please you, really I mean it. But as for "he is scolded," it seems to me that I wrote "we are scolded," not that it pleased me for all that, since it seemed that the person changed without any grace and purpose: perhaps "scolds with sour paternal uncle's words" wouldn't be at all bad.[35] Certainly I wouldn't believe that one used "he is scolded" with active significance. You don't like "confounded peace with gloomy wars" and to me it seemed that I had made a coup in my fashion: so far am I from getting the flavor of what I chirp to myself. I thought I had inserted an argument from Aesop in a few words, the way Horace does: Aesop tells how a good old man used to muddy the waters by fishing every day; and when the neighbors complained, the man said, if he didn't get their waters muddy he wouldn't get his bread: and the interpretation is this, that the rulers in those times stirred up the city so as to divert attention from their life style; and I don't know if I dreamed it, that Aristophanes also used this story. . . .

If I wanted now to get into a "vast sea" of saying how beholden I am that you wrote me in this frank way and again my reasons for speaking badly of those verses, I would make you want to pray to as many saints as you have in your churchlet, right up to the one who holds his head in his hand, that never again would I get this urge to compose and comment: enough that I have to make you a swarm of curtsies and I'll be equal with Pandolfo.[36] I'll wait to write some *Capitoli*, that with less effort come out better, are easy to learn, and stick in the mind.[37]

Geri's questions stem from the interest he shared with Casa in writing Latin. The exchange shows how carefully Casa read Horace and sought to emulate even a manner of compressed allusion: the gist of a Greek fable in one phrase. Closing, like Horace, with playful irony, Casa's parody of prayer moves him back towards the world of the Sirens. *Capitoli*, being obscene verses like Berni's, imply a distinctive manner in literature and life. Calling them easier, both for him to make and for

---

[35] Coined here and kept. It appears in the version finally printed by Petrus Victorius, ed., *Ioannis Casae Latina Monimenta* (Florence: Giunta, 1564); *CL* 3.21.

[36] Casa's sister's son, under Geri's tutelage.

[37] Casa (Rome) to Geri (Bologna: Predalbino), 5 August 1535, *Opere* (1806) 4:354–56.

others to read and remember, Casa makes an unwitting prophecy: his *capitoli* would be recalled and used to thwart the curial ambition he had as yet scarcely conceived.

Fleeing moralistic Latin for Italian scurrility, Casa paused midway for an epigram, still Latin, but scurrilous in the manner of Martial and Catullus, sent to Geri in February 1536 with a note:[38] "I am far from the Muses this year, and good riddance; because they were harmful to me and others." With his usual remorse and frankness, he meditates on freedom from hypocrisy: better a meager poet than a philosopher, though he has the *Ethics* of Aristotle in his hands, he says, and inserts the epigram:

> Quintia, known well to the Roman folk as a whore,
>   whom they call the portico concierge,
> on whom most days the sailors, on holidays the country
>   crowd, wear out their hearty parts:
> perish if she's compared with old-time priests,
>   as chaster and more honest than Ulysses' spouse.
> Yet, gifts she freely gives a boy and, when she sees
>   him gape for eager men, so many in one night,
> "This bed", she says "this stool and feeble lamp,
>   the armor of my art, you, boy, my better, take."[39]

The version pleases less than a previous one, he says, but should placate Geri's appetite for verse. He reproaches Geri for wanting to keep Bembo abreast of all his silliness: "when you can make Bembo believe I have always known and worshipped his divine talent and other excellences, so His Lordship may know from this that I am not always silly and mad."

Again, the recklessness astounds. After deploying Horace and Bembo for his moral defense, Casa composes a poem in a manner and a genre

---

[38] Casa (Rome) to Geri (Padua), 4 February 1536, *Opere* (1806) 4:356–58.
[39]   *Quintia Romana meretrix bene cognita plebi,*
            Haec, quam custodem fornicis esse ferunt,
        In quam profestis nautae, festisque diebus
            Exercet validum rustica turba latus;
        Dispeream Salio possit collata videri.
            Ni proba, nique Ithaci conjuge casta magis.
        Quin ultro haec puero concedit, et ut videt una
            Tot cupidis illum nocte patere viris;
        'Hunc lectum, hanc' ait 'exiguo cum lumine sellam
            Arma meae melior tu, puer, artis, habe.'

that were among the most scabrous from antiquity, and not too badly. He gets the authenticating details of everyday life, custom and religion; the rhetorical point of metaphor and alliteration in "armor of my art"; and the paradox of high praise for a low figure, whose virtue consists in nobly acknowledging a sexual feat: all treated as a matter of aesthetics more or less satisfying. Yet scandal over homosexuality had forced Berni from Rome in 1523, and Casa himself was accused of pederasty because of one of his Bernesque poems, "On the oven."[40] Geri was about to suffer and die from homosexual rape.

A month later Casa reveals even more clearly how far his mind was split between morality and obsessive passion.[41] He explains why he has trouble being as hospitable as Geri recommends to Priuli:

> Because he is so given over to the spirit, and I am, as Your Lordship knows, but little devoted, and I live in a free style, nor can I all at once give up this long habit of mine: as far as I understand, he and Galeazzo[42] have not yet given up hope for my soul, since I am studying the *Ethics*, which all the same has yielded little fruit in me, so much so that I have sometimes read some good bits in a certain place that I will name to Y. L. [Your Lordship] when we are at Predalbino; suffice it that you would have laughed to see me going up on a roof with the unlucky *Ethics* under my arm; and so that Y. L. may know how little fruit I get from that book, I'll tell you another tale, not without verses, so that my letters won't get read.[43]

He goes on to tell in detail how he bullied and seduced a noblewoman, a foreigner living in Rome and ends by reflecting

> certainly the *Ethics* must not have taught me this incontinence *neque tam impudentem* ἀλαζονείαν [nor such impudent shamelessness]. Nor do I want to tell Y. L. now which worked better to achieve its aim, my verses or the *Ethics*. I'll tell you at Predalbino: that solitude and leisure are in my heart and soul very

---

[40] Santosuosso, *Vita*, 49. Casa answered the accusation in a self-defense, which Vettori did not include in the first edition of Casa's Latin. The defense returns, however, in the last edition, where the editor wished to reassure German boys a century and a half later that not only the style but the character of Casa merited their emulation in school: Gundlingius, *Ioannis Casae Latina Monimenta*, 5–6.

[41] Casa (Rome) to Geri (Padua), 2 March 1536, *Opere* (1806) 4:359–61.

[42] Galeazzo Florimonte (ca. 1478–1567).

[43] Casa (Rome) to Geri (Padua), 11 March 1535, *Opere* (1806) 4:349–50.

often, and if my situation did not depend so much on Fortune, I would promise Y. L. a decade, indeed would start to count from '36 [1536]. I don't know anything else to promise that I desire to the highest degree.

Not even his mockery of philosophy prepares for the cynicism with which Casa describes his machinations against the woman, driving the point home by making light of the *Ethics*. Only then does his mind turn once again to the country for escape.

Fortune preempted the decade and put off the desired retreat. The election in 1534 of Paul III had set off a scramble for appointments. Casa discouraged Geri from trying because, he said, the new pope was too old to be courted,[44] which is just what Casa managed to do, finally getting into papal service in 1537. Nowhere does he show awareness of an episode that must have cast its shadow over his new links with power. Pier Luigi Farnese (1503–1547), the father of Cardinal Alessandro and son of Pope Paul, brutally raped Geri. The handsome young bishop of Fano died in 1537, two years after Casa advised him to expect no advantage from Pier Luigi's father and just when Casa was beginning his own climb.[45]

By 1544, when Casa had risen to the archbishopric and was serving as ambassador to Venice, Carlo Gualteruzzi had become secretary to Cardinal Farnese. The communications from the new ambassador to his patron's secretary reflect their long intimacy and color the discussions of papal and Farnese affairs. Sometimes the young cardinal enters into the spirit of play.

Casa's first reports show that rank and responsibility did not cancel his old self:[46] he arrived safe, made short work of the public ceremonies, acted brusque and brief as usual; heard from Bembo, who was quite comfortable as his guest in Rome, as Casa was in the house of Bembo's Venetian friends:

> Quirino, the male, that is, since the female I have yet to see; and Mr Flaminio nearly stops me by a show of pious love, reminding me with what great honor and seriousness an ambassador must behave, and that it is not fitting to steal the beloved from your

---

[44] Casa (Rome) to Geri [Padua], 5 August 1535, *Opere* (1806) 4:354–56.

[45] Giovanna Solari, *The House of Farnese: A Portrait of a Great Family of the Renaissance*, trans. Simona Morini and Frederick Tuten (New York: Doubleday, 1968), 37.

[46] Casa (Venice, as ambassador of the Pope) to Gualteruzzi (Rome, as secretary of Cardinal Farnese), 20 September 1544, *Opere* (1806) 4:178.

neighbor. But I am not about to believe him in either the one or the other.

Sacred language, as ever, gets hijacked by wit. For both Flaminio and Casa Elizabeth Quirini was the object of purely poetic love.

Busy with letters and negotiations, often unwell, Casa insisted that he was slow, even rude, in response to the kindness and generosity of "the magnificent" Elizabeth. Yet he did find time to keep up and extend his old literary habits:

> Verses not to be seen by anyone but the Cardinal and Mr Flaminio;[47]

> My Lady Elizabeth last evening took the *canzona* [sic] from me, so I can't send it to you, but I believe that you will see it; and I warn you, by the love of God, that no one see it but you, my Lords;[48]

> I am amazed that Cardinal Farnese asked for the *canzone*, because His Most Reverend Lordship was not supposed to know I had made it; and may God will that it not be circulated and bring us blame, both as poet and as ambassador, because it is bad poetry, and poetry itself does not suit this other art. . . . I kiss the hand of the Most Reverend My Lord Bembo for the good office and favor . . . ;[49]

> It pains me that I hear the sonnet on the portrait [of Casa by Titian] has been circulating around Rome: and I sent it to no one but you, and then I changed it in a thousand places that were not right before nor are they now.[50]

> I've gotten into a labyrinth of translating certain things from Greek to Latin, and thus I need to make a truce with the Muses and Titian; although I am also being dunned by my creditors, with whom by now I have need of intercessors, since I have been so long in arrears.[51]

The Venetian Bembo of course figures even more prominently than

---

[47] 1 January 1545, *Opere* (1806) 4:198.
[48] 5 February 1545, *Opere* (1806) 4:201.
[49] 15 August 1545, *Opere* (1806) 4:211.
[50] 22 October 1545, *Opere* (1806) 4:210.
[51] 26 November 1545, *Opere* (1806) 4:212. Literary debt had been cited as a reason to write *Il Cortegiano* by Baldassare Castiglione: Saccone, *Le buone e le cattive maniere*, 19–20.

before. He has been elevated to cardinal by Pope Paul and is not only settled in Casa's Rome apartment but the beneficiary of a loan of 300 *scudi* from his host.[52] Casa rarely fails to remind Gualteruzzi to convey regards: "Kiss me the hand of His Very Reverend Lordship, since a Cardinal you cannot simply greet." Casa knows the dignity he seeks. On one occasion Bembo provides the diplomat a moment of opportune access to the head of the Venetian state: the old Doge reminisces about the days when he and Bembo were young together, back in the '90s.

The following spring that other old friend Lodovico Beccadelli went to nearby Trent to assume the position of secretary to the ecumenical council. Casa wrote him in terms that document both their intimacy, the checkered pattern of their lives as humanists, courtiers and clerics, and Casa's perennial generosity with friends:

> One won't play anymore at "Find How Many Things Either Spit or Straw Is Good For," but "For How Many Trades Is Beccadelli Employed" and in how many has he turned out marvelously: carver, majordomo, secretary, reader, brother's keeper, companion of study, poet, physician and president of the Council. Now let Your Lordship go off and reform once and for all this poor deformed Church! and on my behalf kiss the hand of those Most Reverend and Most Illustrious Lords Delegates, and of the Most Reverend of Trent; nor let yourself lack either money or anything else I have, and be well.[53]

In February 1547 Cardinal Bembo died, leaving his intimates in Venice and Rome to squabble over who would publish what among his remaining works. Casa sought to mediate through lengthy and trenchant letters. He offered himself as editor, commented on the typography and layout for the poems and on the arrangement. His insistence on respecting any order Bembo intended bespeaks his own sense of the importance of arrangement in a sequence of poems. He defended Bembo's mannered style in Latin and Italian against the grumbling of Venetian counsellors, who were wary whether such language in Bembo's *History of Venice* would represent the Serene Republic to advantage.[54] Bembo in his last sonnet passed the poetic torch to Casa,[55] and the issues that arose over

---

[52] Santosuosso, *Vita*, 66, quotes a letter from Bembo (Rome) to Girolamo Quirini (Venice), 3 August 1544, showing that Bembo had the run of Casa's vineyard as well as his apartment.

[53] 18 April 1545, *Opere* (1806) 4:371.

[54] Letters to Gualteruzzi during 1547 and 1548, *Opere* (1806) 4:246–319.

[55] Saccone, *Le buone e le cattive maniere*, 126. See Casa's ecstatic reaction and the revis-

his publication prefigure the posthumous fate of Casa's own works:

> The magnificent Quirina so far as I can grasp would want the sonnets left in the order that the Cardinal gave them; and surely, since his Most Reverend Lordship thoughtfully deliberated this order, as I understand, changing it will have need of an excuse, for which the responsibility will fall on you; and I think that you already wrote me something or other about it, and I didn't look at it, not knowing that the Cardinal wanted one order more than another: thus think what is better. And be well.[56]

> As for printing, I leave it to whatever Quirini writes: I mean printing the works of Cardinal Bembo, of good and best memory; and as for my things in Italian, for that I do not believe Your Lordship advised me to print them, still less in company with those of His Most Reverend Lordship; for that you will please wait till they are more and better, and thus I say also for my works in Latin. May our Lord God keep you.[57]

Casa distinguishes between Italian and Latin works and strikes his by now familiar pose of reticence about their divulgation.

Two years passed before the turbulence that spurred the *Carminum Liber*. Pope Paul died on November 10, 1549. Shortly afterwards Casa returned to Rome. In a long and tumultuous conclave, the succession nearly passed to Reginald Cardinal Pole (1500–1558), the brilliant and pious Englishman who had been friendly with Casa since their studies together at Padua. Pole's loyalty to Rome had cost the lives of his mother and brother, executed in revenge by Henry VIII. The new pope, Julius III, urged Casa to go as ambassador to the court of France, but he begged off since his poor health made the journey seem too arduous. Pope Julius soon fell into a territorial dispute with the Farnese clan, Casa's cardinal-patron and his brother Ottavio. Their grandfather Pope Paul had ceded Piacenza and Parma from the papal states to their father, Pier Luigi. The latter, as arrogant and brutal as ever, had been assassinated and his body thrown into the street in 1547, ten years after the rape and death of Cosimo Geri.

The cardinal found it opportune to withdraw to Florence, leaving

---

ions of his response in letters to Gualteruzzi, August and September 1546, *Opere* (1806) 4:237.

[56] 28 January 1548, *Opere* (1806) 4:285.

[57] 29 September 1548, *Opere* (1806) 4:311–12. For the edition that appeared, see the POSTSCRIPT to the Notes and Commentary.

Casa's nearest remaining ties in Rome with the household of Cardinal Pole. He and his closest companions figure in the first two poems of the *Liber*. The censorious Priuli had long been Pole's secretary, and Flaminio had lived with them since 1541. During his final illness, Flaminio addressed the grieving Priuli in a poem pieced together out of Catullan tags: he says that unity of study and of will have made them one in spirit; one dwelling kept, one table nourished them; and he urges Priuli not to grieve too much but rather rejoice that soon they will be reunited in heaven.[58] The Christian sentiments ring strangely in the pastiche of phrases from old Roman eroticism. Although Flaminio imagines his Christian soul in the "blessed dwellings of the sky," Casa summons his "shades" from the pagan afterlife—"Elysian Fields"—in the elegy that opens the *Liber* (*CL* I.1).

Flaminio died in Pole's arms on March 19, 1550, after receiving the last rites from Giovanni Pietro Cardinal Carafa, who as Pope Paul IV after 1555 questioned the orthodoxy of both Pole and Flaminio. Pole arranged for burial in the chapel of the venerable English college.[59]

Meanwhile, the central figure of the elegy was entering the Roman scene. Galeazzo Florimonte had long urged Casa to absorb the lessons of Aristotle's *Ethics*. Flaminio described him affectionately as "This philosopher of ours ... Peripatetic [sc. Aristotelian] in speaking and composing dialogues, and sometimes also a most stern and unbearable Stoic, but in daily life a most delicious and pleasant Epicurean."[60] Galeazzo was serving as bishop of the poor diocese of Aquino when early in 1550 the new pope called him to Rome, making him papal secretary in the fall. This shift from diocesan to curial work ran counter to the tenets of reform favored by Pole, Priuli, and Flaminio, as well as Galeazzo himself. He and Flaminio had belonged to the entourage of Gian Matteo Giberti (1495-1543),[61] who had redeemed a disastrous experience in curial diplomacy by making himself a model pastor as Bishop of Verona from 1528 until his death. Giberti represented an ideal for reformers who favored actual residence and pastoral activity by bishops.

---

[58] *Carm.* VI.36: *Marci Antonii Joannis Antonii et Gabrielis Flaminiorum Forocorneliensium Carmina*, 2 vols. (Prati: Typis Raynerii Guasti, 1831), reprinting the edition by F. M. Mancurtius (Padua: Cominus, 1727).

[59] About this time Ubaldino Bandinelli also died, and Casa came into possession of his books. The list, with note of consignment dated 23 May, 1551, and written by Erasmo Gemini, Casa's secretary, survives in Codex Vaticanus Latinus 14826, 162v-163r.

[60] 11 November 1538: cited by Claudio Scarpati, *Studi sul Cinquecento italiano* (Milan: Università Cattolica del Sacro Cuore, 1982), 148, n. 48.

[61] A. Prosperi, *Tra Evangelismo e Controriforma G. M. Giberti (1495-1543)* (Rome, 1969), xvii, 299, 304, 308, 325-27.

Casa's elegy, then, brings three old friends together in an argument over the clergy's proper role. When Pope Julius called Galeazzo from his diocese to serve in court, Galeazzo's own reformist credentials provoked his friend Priuli to twit him for betraying the example of Giberti.[62] In reply, Casa employs pastoral allegory to defend Galeazzo for answering the call of the "chief shepherd" (read "pope" and "papal court").[63] Casa defends the shift to curial work since it parallels his own preference.

In the next poem, Casa shifts from pastoral allegory to explicit moralism and from elegy to satire, confessing his own sin of ambition to Galeazzo (*CL* II). Casa ends by begging Pole and Priuli to help push him out of Rome, much as he used to appeal for moral guidance to other upright friends. Meanwhile, writing to Beccadelli in Venice, Casa speaks of renouncing ambition for something like the literary retreat they had shared when very young: he reports selling his clerical office as preface to the more tranquil life he now says he has "always" desired.[64] Such a retreat was the pastoral and Petrarchan dream Casa revealed to the unfortunate Geri—a decade of "solitude and leisure" in the country, a flight of fancy while stewing in the Roman summer, plotting and hoping for Fortune to open the way to preferment. Fifteen years later, despair pushes him to realize the dream.

As he vacillates in Rome, Bembo's example haunts him with its success both literary and ecclesiastical.[65] Casa writes Bembo's life, lauding him for a freedom from ambition that Bembo in reality did not practice.[66] In the same spirit, Casa resurrects the epistle (*CL* III) that idealized Bembo's philosophical and poetic equilibrium. Its polemic against vulgar and vicious ambition sets the stage for the polemic against women that Casa translated from Euripides and placed next in the *Liber* (*CL* IV). Once again classical allusion serves to amplify and aim resentment against the female gender: the Euripidean rhetoric permits a veritable paroxysm.

---

[62] G. Biadego, "Galeazzo Florimonti e il *Galateo* di Monsignor della Casa," *Atti Reale Istituto Veneto* 60, 2 (1900): 547–50. See also G. Alberigi, *I Vescovi Italiani al Concilio di Trento (1545–1547)* (Florence, 1959), 225–29 and Casa, *Opere*, comm. G. Verdani (Venice: A. Pasinelli, 1752), 260–61, 273.

[63] Dino Cantimori, "Italy and the Papacy," in *The Reformation 1520–1555*, ed. G. R. Elton, *New Cambridge Modern History* (Cambridge: Cambridge University Press, 1990), 2:257–58.

[64] 9 August 1550, *Opere* (1806) 4:376. Cf. Saccone, *Le buone e le cattive maniere*, 123.

[65] Saccone, *Le buone e le cattive maniere*, 124–26.

[66] *Le buone e le cattive maniere*, 124.

The rising waves of blame spill over into a decision to leave Rome, which Casa expresses in epode form (*CL* V), taking a leaf from Horace, whose second epode told of a miser leaving urban greed for simple rural life only to lapse from the ideal within the month.

Casa's actual departure was delayed by the need to look out for interests of his nephews and by one of his debilitating attacks of gout (spring 1551).[67] By fall he managed to get to Venice. His first steps are not as well documented as when he became ambassador. Only in the next year do letters begin to show how he employed his retreat.

A letter in March 1552 to Astorre Paleotti, who had been a friend since student days and was then with Cardinal Farnese in Florence, shows that separate exiles had, if anything, intensified relations between the patron and the poet. The pope had ordered Casa to join the council in Trent, and he had demurred:

> If His Beatitude persists, I will obey with much inconvenience to my body and my spirit and thus I will abandon the odes and poorly will I be able to serve My Lord our most illustrious patron with the ode that His Most Reverend Lordship desires on the variability of Fortune; besides that, since so noble a poet as is Horace beyond the Greeks, has spoken of this matter, I would be considered rash to get into it; still if I have the leisure I will see to saying at my convenience some simplicities to content the cardinal.
>
> If I had had so much spirit, I would have sent my ode on flattery [burn damage to manuscript] ... that I sent, since in any case it came into the hands of His Most Reverend Lordship and is [burn damage to manuscript] ... for what I see circulates and I send you a copy of it; as for the comparison of the stepmother, I wanted to say this: "Flattery knows how to destroy the credulous mind no differently than stepmothers when wickedly they mask, as of old, deadly dishes with heaps of honey"; the which comparison would be complete and entire if I had said besides: "know how to destroy stepsons." This comparison as I put it was praised a good deal by my Roman friends.[68]

Casa has used his leisure to take up writing odes, acutely aware that he

---

[67] Casa (Rome) to Beccadelli (Venice), 25 April 1551, *Opere* (1806) 4:380.
[68] Casa (Venice) to Astorre Paleotti (Florence, in the house of Cardinal Farnese), Santosuosso, "Inediti casiani," 493–94.

risks comparison with the Roman master of the genre. As for the theme requested, it was only too timely: Fortune had made Casa's patron a teenage cardinal, propelling Casa towards the purple, and now had set both back. For the ode on Fortune requested by his patron, Casa adopts the meter used by Horace in dedicating his book to his (*Carm.* I.1). As for the theme of dangerous flattery, plenty of it had come the cardinal's way, not least from poets like Flaminio and Molza. Casa's ode against flattery (*CL* VII) might have been composed before he left Rome. He addressed it to his nephew Annibale, who had been at the center of his attention as he prepared to go, and he says that it won the approval of his Roman friends. Yet he also wrote Annibale when he could no longer speak directly, and he would certainly keep up his lifelong habit of sending verses for comment.

Further light on the Latin poems comes from a letter only two days later to Pier Vettori:

> Since I have more leisure and a bit more health than usual, I set myself to reread the Poets, mostly the Greeks, put aside by me for a long time; and reading them there came made to me some Latin verses, as Your Lordship has seen, although my verses were not written for you and your equals (if you have for that any equals), but for Cosenzans and such like, and for this reason I never desired to send you them.[69]

Casa speaks of writing poetry in curiously impersonal language: *mi è venuto fatto dei versi* (to me there came made some verses). He gives no sign of motivation from anywhere but poetry itself, nor does he identify the genre, although a turn of phrase betrays one presence in his mind: *intermessi da me lungo tempo* (long put aside) resembles Horace's signal of returning to write odes at the start of his fourth book: *intermissa, Venus, diu rursus bella moves* (Venus, you stir again wars long put aside, *Carm.* IV.1.1). Casa's excuse, that he did not write for the likes of Vettori, would have at least specious plausibility if the poem in question were the flattery ode for his nephew.

Less than a week later, Casa writes that, since his Latin verses are getting around, he prefers Vettori to get them from him directly, "so I have had made for you a copy of what I am writing (*quel ch'io scrivo*) in memory of Mons. Ubaldino" (*CL* VI).[70]

---

[69] 2 March 1552, *Opere* (1806) 4:158.
[70] 9 March 1552, *Opere* (1806) 4:160.

The ode on Ubaldino Bandinelli leads off a cycle of odes in the *Carminum Liber* and strongly confirms Casa's preoccupation with Horace, yet the letter implies that it is work in progress at a time when the flattery ode (*CL* VII) had already circulated, inspiring Vettori's interest and Farnese's request for a Fortune ode. The absolute chronology of the first two odes thus remains uncertain, all the more so given Casa's penchant for revision. In them he does opt for a family of Horatian meters that he carries over into odes demanded by the cardinal, both on Fortune (*CL* VIII) and on Cardinal de Tournon (*CL* IX), and eventually into an ode on Vettori himself (*CL* XIII).

Ten months pass. At the end of January, 1553, Casa expresses pleasure that Vettori thinks so well of Cardinal Farnese, indeed is guiding him in study.[71] Recalling the cardinal's long affection and aid, glossing over the disappointments, he asks Vettori to "kiss his hands in my name: which [sc. hands] could yet one day honorably free from the mill his friend, who has nearly finished the task; which, if it be recalled to him occasionally, he will do."

What task had been assigned and what Casa meant by the metaphor of enslavement and getting free from the mill comes out after six more months. In July, 1553, he writes Vettori as if mentioning Latin poetry for the first time:

> I got into an unnecessary nuisance, that is of making Latin verse, and I believed I could free myself from it on my own terms, but the opposite befalls me, not only because I myself can't keep myself away from it so easily, but also because sometimes I am sought to make them by persons, to whom I am not eager to say no, such as Cardinal Farnese and some others. But I see, then, that their contentment is my shame in two ways: one, because to be a Poet is not perhaps compatible with my rank; and the other, because to be a bad Poet is not compatible with any rank.[72]
>
> I have made an ode at the urging of Cardinal Farnese in praise of Madame Margaret, the sister of the king of France, or rather said that the ode ought to be made, as Y. L. will see, since I am sending it to you (*CL* XI). Y. Lord. has in great part the blame, that I am sought, because you gave me a reputation with H. Most Illustrious Lord. both in speaking and writing: be content, then, to take the

---

[71] Casa (Venice) to Vettori (Florence), 27 January 1553, *Opere* (1806) 2:201-3.

[72] A variant of this argument appeared in a letter written during the ambassadorship and cited above: 15 August 1545, *Opere* (1806) 4:211.

trouble to see it, and to read it two times, and freely advise me in general, and in particular, without any reserve; because my nature is to change, and to rechange, and willingly to remake again, like one who has no haste. I have not given out this ode, and I will not give it unless I hear first the opinion of Y. L., but the cardinal has had me pressured for it a great deal.

I was also forced to write another in praise of Cardinal Tournon, which has more sinew than this; but the times don't allow me to send it.[73]

Behind the metaphors of enslavement lay the reality of serving a patron: the hopes of advantage and the actual pressure to perform. Casa had met Cardinal Farnese's request for the Fortune ode with an ironical promise of "simplicities." A different tone is needed to satisfy the interests of his family at the French court. The resulting ode can hardly have delighted the cardinal with its implicit plea that the experience of a career under his patronage had left Casa too corrupted to write ennobling verse (CL XI). The ode on Cardinal de Tournon also paid a Farnese debt (CL IX). The French prelate had brilliantly carried off an apparently impossible diplomatic mission the previous spring (1552), advancing Farnese interests. With mingled cajolery, deceit, and threats he persuaded Julius III to abandon his alliance with the emperor and ally himself with the French in support of the Farnese hold on Piacenza.[74]

After writing on July 15 for Vettori's help, Casa retreated to the country. Already by August 12 he is back in Venice and thanking Vettori for a prompt and encouraging reply that praised the questioned ode (CL XI).[75] Casa promises to make any future adjustments Vettori may suggest, "since now I have no other business that entertains me more than coddling myself with literature." He adds that the Cardinal Sant'Angelo (Ranuccio Farnese [1530-1565], younger brother of Alessandro) has carried off a copy of the ode just as it is, but this will not keep him from further improvements if he can make them. Neither Vettori nor Casa himself comments on the personal confession, the ode's almost hysterical cry that Rome and curial ambition had left an unredeemable blemish. Yet these are themes that emerge, too, in the powerful *canzone*

---

[73] 15 July 1553, *Opere* (1806) 2:175-76.

[74] De Tournon's shifting fortunes and ultimate triumph are described in detail by Michel François, *Le Cardinal François de Tournon, Homme D'État, Diplomate, Mécène e Humaniste (1489-1562)* (Paris: E. de Boccard, 1951), 239-89.

[75] 12 August 1553, *Opere* (1806) 2:200.

"Errai gran tempo" (I strayed a long time) (*Rime* XLVII), where Casa decries his failed ambitions in love, in the curia, and in letters.

By September, the nervousness subsides.[76] Casa thanks Vettori for a book and congratulates him on the style and tact of its dedicatory epistle to Cardinal Farnese. He poses a question about the theodicy of Lucretius and concludes, almost as an afterthought, that he is calmly reading the poets, which takes longer than he expected. It sounds as if he has moved from Greek to Latin poets in an extension of the project he undertook when his exile began.

In February of the following year, Casa writes from the country to Beccadelli in Venice that he has put aside the poets in order to concentrate on writing the life of Gasparo Cardinal Contarini, the pious Venetian reformer.[77] At the end of March, however, he is telling Vettori:

> I am sending an ode to Y. L. made by me with much affection of the spirit, if only so were it made with much art and much adequacy; if it seems to you that I should change anything, I pray you to advise me freely.[78]

The ode to Vettori (*CL* XIII) varies the Asclepiadean meters of the first odes and introduces themes of exile's harshness and having harvested enough. Casa thus not only closes the cycle of odes but hints at the end of retirement itself: these themes and their placement corroborate what he wrote in February to Beccadelli about winding down his engagement with Latin verse.

From Vettori, the ode elicited an outpouring of gratitude and praise that Casa parried in his next letter with further praise of his friend and deprecation of himself.[79] He begs forgiveness for not replying sooner to Vettori's "very sweet letters": some visitors kept him "busy and tied up," he says, and he asked the abbott (at the monastery in Narvesa where he retreated in the country) to write Vettori on his behalf and send him "an ode that Cardinal Farnese *mi ha fatto fare* (made me make)."

This description could fit three of the poems documented by the letters: the ode to Margaret of France (*CL* XI) ordered by the cardinal almost exactly one year earlier;[80] the Fortune ode (*CL* VIII) earlier still;

---

[76] Casa (Di Villa in Trevisana) to Vettori (Florence), 25 September 1553, *Opere* (1806) 2:211–13.
[77] 13 February 1554, *Opere* (1806) 4:381–82.
[78] 31 March 1554, *Opere* (1806) 4:164.
[79] 16 July 1554, *Opere* (1806) 2:207–8.
[80] 15 July 1553, *Opere* (1806) 2:175–76.

and the ode on de Tournon (*CL* IX), who did so much to confirm the Farnese usurpation. Most probably Casa forgot his whole earlier exchange over the ode to Margaret and had it sent again, much as once before he had forgotten sending the Bandinelli ode.

Self-conscious irony about his poetic powers continues at the beginning of September. The gout, he says, likes especially to torment "more than any other part the fingers that write, perhaps wanting to warn me, albeit late, to let be the art that I don't know how to practice."[81]

The self-irony echoes nearly five months later.[82] Casa dreams of attending Vettori's lectures on Pindar and Aeschylus: "and certainly I need it, having sometimes had the name of Poet, albeit wrongly; I ought to know them and remember them much better than I do. But I would like the lesson to be read in this leisure and tranquillity in Venice, to which Your Lordship is invited and desired and awaited by me most highly." Casa offers Vettori hospitality and financial help if hard times find him in want. He concludes: "With all these noises of war I have spent five months in this quiet, where the greatest disturbance I have are the bells, that sometimes don't let me think." This is his only reference to the subject that became his theme of closure for the *Carminum Liber* in the final epigrams (*CL* XIV–XVI).

Retirement was about to end. In Casa's last letter, written towards the end of April,[83] the talk turns from poetry to the world: health, he says, will keep him in the country for the summer; again he invites Vettori to take refuge with him. Yet he also speaks of being constrained to go to Benevento, the diocese he had still not seen, and of another duty, to kiss the feet of the new pope. Following the death of Julius III (March 23, 1555), his successor Paul IV, the same Cardinal Carafa who attended Flaminio's death, restored Cardinal Farnese to influence. The occasion tempted Vettori, who joined the scramble for office and rushed to Rome. If he banked on the relationship established with Farnese during the latter's Florentine exile, he was disappointed. Casa diplomatically assures him that he would be well received by the cardinal and fortunate to be a guest in such a house; he offers his own good offices if they can serve.

It was Casa who got the nod. Despite his health, he was called to

---

[81] 1 September 1554, *Opere* (1806) 2:178.

[82] Casa (Trevisana) to Vettori (Florence), 23 January 1555, *Opere* (1806) 4:166–68.

[83] Casa ("Di villa sul Trevisano") to Vettori (Rome), 26 April 1555, *Opere* (1806) 4:168–69.

Rome to fill the office of papal secretary. To Vettori back in Florence, a letter came in late July from Casa's nephew Annibale Rucellai explaining what had occurred:[84] there was an uproar in the court because "all or the greater part of the ministers of Our Lord were proposed by or dependents of Farnese, so that even some were removed of those who were already set and in place, on which account it did not seem possible to the cardinal to propose still others." Rucellai assures Vettori of the cardinal's esteem, and that he will also have Casa's support if occasion presents itself: Casa, he adds, "has not had time to be able to write two verses to Y. L., still less answer you; and prays you to forgive him until he can make up the lack as he would like to do."

The moment for poetry was past. Yet sometime in the year before returning to Rome, Casa composed another ode. It had been July 16, 1554, when he mentioned the abbott's sending the ode "that Cardinal Farnese made me make." Two days later Orazio Farnese, yet another brother of the cardinal, was killed defending Hesdin in Flanders against imperial siege. In honor of the young duke, Casa produced an ode (*CL* XII); when and under what circumstances is not clear. The choice of meter and the address to the widow do suggest that he took into account not only political opportunity but formal and thematic coherence among his odes.

As late as November, Casa speaks well of another's poem commemorating the death.[85] His remark comes incidentally in the context of an exchange of literary compliments about odes on Cardinal de Tournon: Casa's ode on the cardinal (*CL* IX) had been conveyed to its subject, inspiring a congratulatory letter from the cardinal's secretary, Denis Lambin, the noted scholar. Lambin sent a poem of his own on de Tournon, along with another on the dead duke. Casa replied with effusive compliments. He deprecated his own ode for de Tournon by comparison with Lambin's, allowing that his poor Muse need not have made the journey to France, carrying "timber to the woods" (*in sylvam enim ligna scilicet*): "with very loving letters and a very serious and sweet poem you have stirred and inflamed my love for you. That also comes to me from you as most welcome, the fact that deploring in distinguished verses the wretched fall of Orazio Farnese you have

---

[84] Rucellai (Rome) to Vettori (Florence), 20 July 1555, Santosuosso, "Le opere," 47, British Library Ms. Add. 10272, fol. 9r–v.

[85] Casa (Venice?) to Denis Lambin (Lyon?), 13 November 1554, *Opere*, comm. G. B. Casotti (Florence: G. Mannin, 1707) 3:274.

celebrated him with divine praises." He goes on to speak admiringly of the Farnese brothers and proudly recount his long, close ties to them, giving no sign that he, too, might have written or be intending to write on the duke's death.

If a hint was needed, it came emphatically from a fellow Florentine, Giovanni Battista Amalteo, who composed a grandiloquent ode urging Casa to return from a lofty poetic journey and to memorialize the young Farnese with an ode in the tradition of Greek Alcaeus (and, by inference, the Latin Horace), which is the form employed by Amalteo himself.[86] The metaphor of the poetic journey is a commonplace but one that Casa employed boldly in his ode for de Tournon (*CL* IX), which described itself metaphorically as an ambitious trip across the Alps (the trip that in reality he refused to undertake when he declined to go as ambassador to France). Casa's Florentine admirer pours fulsome eulogy on Casa's poetic mission and Farnese's heroism, so that the poem in effect becomes what it recommends: an ode in Alcaic verse honoring the dead duke. Exactly halfway through the poem a strophe invokes Casa in heroic terms:

> *At tu beato carmine principem*
> *Stellis reponens tu iuuenis memor*
> *caliginosis exime umbris,*
> *Magne Casa, egregios triumphos.* (57–60)

(But you who place with blessed song the prince
    among the stars, you, mindful of the youth,
    redeem from murky shades,
    great Casa, his outstanding triumphs.)

The hint bids fair to exhaust the theme. Yet Casa excogitates an original approach of his own, aided by the developing coherence of his book: he seizes on the opportunity to follow the Margaret ode (*CL* XI) with a second address to a French princess, once more in an apposite meter of Horace. The existence of the book aids and guides him in fulfilling the unexpected task.

In the end, the book imposed itself. It suggested opportune strategy for politic odes (*CL* VI, VIII, IX, XI, XII, XIII), and it occasioned the paradoxical closing epigrams as well as a more than Horatian meditation on its own measured poetics (*CL* X). The book also brought back with

---

[86] Casotti, reprinted from *Opere* (1707) in *Opere* (1806) 1:83.

renewed effect the epistle written years before and allowed the occasional polemic of the opening elegy to acquire new weight: anchoring the frame of the book and justifying Casa's own impending movement from the country to the city.

The elegy lost its original point when Galeazzo left the curia for pastoral work in 1552, going to his home town of Sessa as bishop. But if the quarrel with Priuli became history, its themes haunted Casa as he edged away from rural retreat, thought momentarily of pastoral duty in Benevento, and yearned for Rome. The issues transcended the rather narrow first occasion, keeping the elegy fresh in Casa's mind and recommending it as the cornerstone of his book. A specific link was the name "Galateus," which served in the elegy's defense of Galeazzo as a country sage with healing hands for urban ills. The name and figure served again in the treatise on manners, with its fictional narrator an old rustic "Galateo." Casa's compliment to Galeazzo reflects their two decades of philosophical friendship. Galeazzo had urged the *Ethics* on Casa and was preparing a dialogue on Aristotle's moral philosophy, a leading part of which is the doctrine of the mean that so preoccupied Casa's thought[87]—avoidance of extremes for the middle way. This Aristotelian and Horatian ideal permeates the *Galateo* and the *Carminum Liber* even as it eluded Casa in life.[88]

As the name "Galateo" became identified with the treatise and its narrator, this new literary presence eclipsed the original association. The allegory in the elegy shifted reference. Before it pointed to a certain old bishop under attack by a specific poem. Now it suggests a literary work prepared in the country but meant to benefit the city. The latter reflects, too, on Casa as he prepares to leave exile and return to curial service. The details of the original polemic fade, leaving the contrast between city and country and the claim that moral healing from the country may benefit the corrupt city and its rulers. These themes frame the rest of the book.

The thrust of the *Carminum Liber* is more positive than the bitter despair of the *Rime*, as befits the public and aristocratic bias of culture in Latin. Yet the courtly Latin left scant trace, as noted earlier, while the shriller vernacular determined Casa's literary fate.[89]

---

[87] Scarpati, *Studi sul Cinquecento*, 146–51.

[88] Saccone, *Le buone e le cattive maniere*, passim, thoroughly studies Casa's philosophical roots and personal contradictions.

[89] Durling, *Petrarch's Lyric*, 4.

III. The System and Poetics of the Book

In both the lyrics and the *Carminum Liber* Casa produces a unified sequence or poetry book, adopting and adapting practices going back to the *canzoniere* of Petrarch, who in turn had emulated the *Bucolics* of Virgil.[90] Thematically, the lyrics pass from an erotic to an ethical vision, while meeting other criteria for a true sequence, understood as a closed system where reciprocally related parts convey an overall meaning.[91] Likewise, the *Liber* unfolds a thematic conflict between ambition and retreat, while showing other signs of systematic relations among parts that convey a sense of a whole.

Meters, Genres and Models

Poem numbers: Metrical Group	Genre	Main Literary Model
I–III: DACTYLIC		
I elegiac [6 da͜// + 3 da͜͝/3 da͜͝///]	elegy	Catullus and Propertius
II hexameter [6 da͜//]	satire	Horace
III hexameter [6 da͜//]	epistle	Horace
IV–V: IAMBIC		
IV (pure iambics) [3 ia//]	epode	Horace
V (dactylic + iambic) [6 da͜// + 2 ia//]	epode	Horace
VI–XIII: LYRIC		
VI–IX: Asclepiadean		
VI: second type	ode	Horace
VII: third type	ode	Horace
VIII: first type	ode	Horace
IX: second type	ode	Horace
X: Phalaecean	lyric	Catullus, not Horace
XI–XII: Alcaic		
XI:	ode	Horace
XII:	ode	Horace
XIII: Asclepiadean, fifth type	ode	Horace

---

[90] *Petrarch's Lyric*, 7–11.
[91] Silvia Longhi, "Il tutto e le parti nel sistema di un canzoniere (Giovanni della Casa)," *Strumenti Critici* 39–40 (1979): 265, 294–96.

XIV–XVI: DACTYLIC
    XIV [6 da‑// + 3 da‑‑/3 da‑‑///]   epigram   Catullus, not Horace
    XV [6 da‑// + 3 da‑‑/3 da‑‑///]   epigram   Catullus, not Horace
    XVI [6 da‑// + 3 da‑‑/3 da‑‑///]   epigram   Catullus, not Horace

Remarks

CL I: Non-Horatian dactylic verse-form begins the book.

CL II–V: Horatian hexameters and iambics form the cycle of four poems representing Casa's moral crisis and departure from Rome.

CL VI–XIII: Horatian cycle of lyrics from exile looking to return.

CL VI–IX: Horatian poems in Asclepiadean meters, with diverse types succeeding one another and the initial type returning to close.

CL X: Non-Horatian verses articulate Horatian aesthetic for the book.

CL XI–XII: Horatian meter of great public odes in Farnese diptych.

CL XIII: Horatian form returns and varies, with advance to a more complex type, closing the whole set of lyrics.

CL XIV–XVI: Non-Horatian dactylic verse-form encloses and closes the whole book.

Similarities with Horace appear in the cycle of lyric meters (*CL* VI–XIII): varying Asclepiadean types within a sequence,[92] bringing back a type after an interval so as to punctuate or close,[93] using a sharp metrical departure to punctuate and synthesize;[94] doubling the Alcaic strophe,[95] giving it prominence in place and subject;[96] and capping an entire mixed progression with the rare fifth Asclepiad, brought back in an advance to climax with closural effect.[97]

Also Horatian are the satire and epistle (*CL* II, III) and the epodes

---

[92] E.g., *Carm.* I.2–11: see the discussion by Matthew Santirocco, *Unity and Design in Horace's Odes* (Chapel Hill: University of North Carolina Press, 1986), 14–41. The simple sequence of Asclepiad types 3 and 4 occurs three times in the first book; 5 and 6, 14 and 15, 23 and 24. Faced with a confusion of nomenclature for the Asclepiad types, I have opted for the practice that numbers them in the order of their appearance in Horace's first book of odes.

[93] E.g. *Carm.* I.2, 10, 20, 22, 30, 32, 38.

[94] E.g. *Carm.* I.7, 28, or 11, 18; also II.18 and IV.8.

[95] E.g. *Carm.* I.16 and 17, 26 and 27, 34 and 35; II 19 and 20. No other meters are paired in the first or second books. In the third book, Horace pairs once each the Asclepiad type 4 (*Carm.* III.16 and 17) and type 2 (*Carm.* III.24 and 25), but this book opens with the famous run of six poems in Alcaic strophe—the so-called Roman Odes.

[96] E.g. II.13, 14, and 15; 19 and 20; and III.1, 2, 3, 4, 5, and 6, but of course also the two poems naming Augustus that close Book IV.

[97] Casa here carries further what Horace did with this meter at a crucial moment in his first sequence: *Carm.* I.11; cf. discussion by Santirocco, *Unity and Design*, 44–46.

(*CL* IV, V). Also, when Casa announces a poetic program in *CL* X, the sole authority claimed is Horace. Casa professes scorn for the vulgar, as did Horace in the famous opening of his third book of odes, "I hate the profane crowd"; and Casa claims for himself Horace's ideal of a moderation both moral and aesthetic. In short, he navigates by a Horatian sense of variation in meter and theme,[98] also by the Horatian ethical and aesthetic vision that locates "measure" in the "measures" of poetic art and most specifically in the book array.

Yet Casa does not, cannot, confine himself within such measure, either aesthetic or ethical. He overreaches the Horatian mold, much as his lyrics break the measured style of Petrarch and Bembo.[99] Horace confined distinct genres to separate books, never mingling hexameter, epodic, and lyric poetry in one. Nor did Horace even employ the meters that open and close Casa's book or the one that defines its poetics.

For the example of a poetic book mingling genres and reflecting personal crisis, Casa could look to Catullus. In fact, he defends his poetics in a pastiche of Catullan phrases (*CL* X, see notes) compiled in the manner of his friend Flaminio, whose ghost Casa summons in his opening elegy. Casa's call to Flaminio in the underworld brings to mind Catullus's elegies evoking his brother recently dead at Troy (*Carm.* 65.1–8, 68.91–100). Casa's book, then, closes with an echo of Catullus's opening: Catullus contrasted his own slight verses with the massive production of a friend (*Carm.* 1.3–7), while Casa expresses his desire for closure despite incessant bells. Both Catullus's copious friend and the person of the belfry are named Cornelius.

In sum, traces of Catullus point beyond the emulation of Horace, not only in the outer frame (*CL* I, XIV–XVI) and the theoretical program (*CL* X), but even in the too vividly sensual image of the seductive girl (*CL* VIII). Not that Casa therefore rushes to incorporate the full measure of Catullus. He adapts only three Catullan genres, and his book contains not more than a hundred but only sixteen poems, far fewer in number, too, than the prolific Catullan imitations of Flaminio.

Recourse to classical poetry, and indeed to Latin itself, places Casa among the reactionaries of his own day. Yet he adapts his models in a way that parallels his writing in Italian, both his roughening of Petrar-

---

[98] Similar considerations govern the choice of meters in Horatian sequences, as recent studies have emphasized. For an orderly discussion of ordering criteria in ancient poetry books, see Santirocco, *Unity and Design*, 1–13, with comments on meter in the first book of *Odes*, pp. 19–21.

[99] Saccone, *Le buone e le cattive maniere*, 127.

chan style and his deliberately simple prose in *Galateo*. His use of multiple genres to narrate a transformation in his own life and to expose a cycle of themes goes beyond both Catullus and Horace as well as any of his contemporaries. Casa shares the ideological commitment to Rome and to Italy's preeminence often expressed through Latin, yet he uses Latin in a way that transcends and personalizes even those goals, creating a sequence that goes beyond precursors in both ancient and Renaissance tradition.[100]

IV. The History of the Edition

After discovering the *Carminum Liber* in its printed form, I found myself tempted by a question nearly unthinkable in the case of an ancient Greek or Roman writer: might there still survive somewhere an original manuscript written by the author? The hope had some grounds. Numerous manuscripts exist from Casa's hand.

A promising hint appeared in letters to Pier Vettori from Annibale Rucellai, who acted as his uncle's literary executor. Vettori had written to take exception to a slur on Dante's style in the first edition of Casa's Italian works. Rucellai replied in a manner all too like his uncle's, deflecting blame to others—the editors and relatives and friends who had constrained him virtually with violence to agree to publication.[101] Although he had provided room and board in his own house in Venice for several months and given a free hand to Carlo Gualteruzzi for editing, Rucellai professed to find the resulting product hasty and uncritical and to fear a similar fate for the works in Latin. Hence he welcomed an offer by Vettori to review the Latin works before publication. At the year's end Rucellai thanked Vettori for having intervened to keep the Giunta publishing house from mistreating his uncle's Latin writings and for an offer to take them under his own critical wing.[102] Rucellai goes on to express confidence that the embarrassments of the Italian edition

---

[100] Sole, *Cognizione*, 9–12; Saccone, *Le buone e le cattive maniere*, 117. Of another order is the grandiose program in the *Hymni naturales* of Michael Marullus, with their "metrical ποικιλία," discussed by M. J. McGann, "Reading Horace in the Quattrocento: the *Hymn to Mars* of Michael Marullus," in *Homage to Horace: A Bimillenary Celebration*, ed. S. J. Harrison (Oxford: Clarendon Press, 1995), 335, followed by exemplary analysis (338–47) of the "hymn which displays the most vigorous interaction with Horace" (336) even as it reflects on political and religious issues of concern to the poet.

[101] 29 January 1559, Bologna, Santosuosso, "Le opere," 48–49.

[102] 2 December 1559, Rome, Santosuosso, "Le opere," 49–50.

will not be repeated under Vettori's care. The outcome, he predicts, will be excellent, and he promises to help by sending Vettori all that he has, only not at once, since he has the material in Venice but will be tied down in Rome until a new pope is elected.

When Rucellai got to Venice towards the middle of the following year (1560), he wrote Vettori that such works as he found in Latin were mostly in disorder and not easily readable.[103] He ordered copies made in good form and the whole, what little there was, sent to Vettori in Florence. Although Rucellai gives no specifics, these copies must include what Casa was producing in Latin during his retirement (1551–1555). When Casa went back to Rome in 1555 for his troubled months in the papal court and death in 1556, he must have left behind this set of papers along with others. In Venice there were boxes of his uncle's writings (*cassaccie di scritture*), writes Rucellai in another letter. He uses the pejorative suffix that implies disorder and decay through the fog of ceremonious courtesies with which he always addresses Vettori: the copies and record books are lost, he says, and he doubts he can find the letters in Latin that Vettori wants to add to the edition.[104]

Despite the hope raised by Rucellai's account of transcriptions made and sent, no sign of them appears among Vettori's papers in Munich. Whatever Vettori gave to the Giuntas to be printed has been lost. What Munich does provide is evidence for the separate circulation of poems—the brisk literary traffic documented by the letters.

Another trail led to Rome. Besides whatever remained behind in Venice eventually to be copied for Vettori, Casa had some manuscripts, both Latin and Italian, with him in Rome during his final months. When he died in the house of Giovanni Cardinal dei Ricci in Via Giulia, these manuscripts remained in possession of the cardinal's heirs. Only in 1968 did the Vatican Library purchase and restore them, since the acid ink was destroying the paper at many points. None of these manuscripts was available to the first editors of Casa in the years just after his death. Now modern editors are asking whether the versions preserved in Rome or those printed in Venice and Florence represent Casa's last and best word. Most of the controversy has arisen over the most famous work. Among the Vatican papers is a manuscript of the *Galateo* that was carefully produced in the hand of Casa's secretary, Erasmo Gemini de Cesis, with some marginal corrections by Casa himself. In style, the

---

[103] 7 May 1560, Venice, Santosuosso, "Le opere," 50.
[104] 24 March 1564, Santosuosso, "Le opere," 62.

whole is less refined and focused than what Gualteruzzi published in Venice two years after Casa died. Editors disagree which version should represent Casa today, but it is clear that the Vatican copies are the latest that he saw and that they were not available to Gualteruzzi in the north.[105]

As for the *Carminum Liber*, the manuscripts in the Vatican like those in Munich yield no direct evidence. Only the highly political ode for Cardinal de Tournon (*CL* IX) was copied by Casa's secretary in the same careful hand as the *Galateo* and brought to Rome. It had been too controversial to send Vettori in the period when Cardinal Farnese was withdrawn in Florence. Now that Farnese was back in Rome with the ear of a new pope, the poem was singled out to be brought along. The Rome text contains one distinct improvement over what Vettori would print.

In what follows I describe the sources for the poems that appear in the *Carminum Liber* and explain their relationships. They confirm the letters' testimony that Casa frequently revised and that multiple versions circulated.

1564 *Latina monimenta Ioannis Casae*, ed. Pier Vettori (Florence: Bernard Giunta's Sons, 1564).
Adopted as the copy text.

Editing Casa's Latin works, Vettori places first the *Carminum Liber*, no doubt privileging poetry over prose, especially poetry he esteemed,[106] that assigned prominence to his own ode and, above all, served his continuing desire to curry Farnese favor. He sent the published volume to Alessandro Cardinal Farnese in Rome and wrote in an accompanying letter that he found "much praise and glory" of the Farneses in the works, "almost from first to last."[107] Allowing for courtly exaggeration, the *Liber* does give prominence to four odes of special Farnese interest: on Fortune (*CL* VIII), on Cardinal de Tournon (*CL* IX), to Margaret (*CL* XI), and on Orazio Farnese (*CL* XII).

---

[105] Gennaro Barbarisi, ed., *Galateo* (Venice: Marsilio, 1991), 9–21; Arnaldo Di Benedetto, ed., *Se si debba prendere moglie, Galateo*, I classici italiani TEA (Turin: UTET, 1992), 29–32. Both admit the stylistic advance of the first edition over the Vatican manuscript, a difference attributed by Barbarisi to Casa's friends editing his text to save his reputation (18), while Di Benedetto believes that only Casa himself could have achieved such improvements (30), a thesis difficult to square with the state of Casa's mind and health once he left his literary retreat for Rome.

[106] Letters from Venice, 15 July 1553, *Opere* (1806) 2:175–76, and 12 August 1553, *Opere* (1806) 2:200.

[107] 10 June 1564, Florence, Santosuosso, "Le opere," 63.

1563 *Carmina poetarum nobilium studio conquisita*, ed. Johannes Paulus Ubaldinus (Milan: Antonius Antonianus, 1563) 74r–76r.

First printing of three separate odes, in an anthology, not in the order of the sequence: *CL* VIII ("Against Fortune"), *CL* XII ("Death of Orazio Farnese"), and *CL* VII ("To Annibale Rucellai Against Flattery"). For the ode "Against Flattery," Ubaldinus presents a redaction slightly different from Vettori's of 1564, but agreeing with **1560** and a copy in Casa's hand (see **Autograph** below).

1560 *Codex latinus monacensis* 485, "Carmina illustrium poetarum aetate nostra florentium ... Ludovichius Dominichius Federico Fuggero. ... Florentiae 1560"

Manuscript anthology in the Munich Staatsbibliothek, written out by Lodovico Dominichio for Friedrich Fugger, includes the following odes by Casa, again not in the order of Casa's book: *CL* VII ("To his Nephew against Flattery"), *CL* VI ("Praise of his Dead Teacher"), *CL* XI ("Self-blame in Praise of a Princess Royal"), *CL* XIII ("Praise of Vettori"), *CL* VIII ("Against Fortune"). An ode here attributed to Casa, but in fact urging him to memorialize Orazio Farnese (Alcaic strophe) is by Giovanni Battista Amalteo.[108]

The selection includes only odes and only those documented in the letters as having circulated in Florence. *CL* VII occurs in its alternate version (cf. **1563** above and **Autograph** below), not that of **1564**; and the final ode is not even Casa's. Thus Dominichio did not have access to the material sent by Rucellai from Venice and used by Vettori in 1564. Enough copies were loose in Florence that publishers could even plan an edition without Rucellai.

Rome *Codex Vaticanus latinus* 14825, fols. 118–19.

Copy of *CL* IX written by the same hand (Casa's secretary's) as the copies of Bembo's life and the *Galateo* in this binder. One strophe differs markedly from 1564 (see texts below).

Autograph *Codex latinus monacensis* 760, item 77.

An autograph copy of *CL* VII ("His Nephew against Flattery") in the same redaction that appears also in 1560 and 1563 (see texts below).

---

[108] Casotti, reprinted from *Opere* (1707) in *Opere* (1806) 1:83.

Some of the principal variant readings just mentioned are reproduced below, enough to show how irregularly they are distributed among the sources.

CL VII,17-26.

1564:
    Sensus <u>vt</u> iuueni pellicit intimos
        Virgo candida, cum turgidulas tegens
        Nulla ueste papillas
        Molli illum recipit sinu,   20
    <u>Sic</u> laudes animum, uera ubi concinunt,
        Permulcere solent. Nec mulier tamen
        Vt cantu sine dulcis
        <u>Spernit</u> psallere tibiae   24
    Sic virtus populus, si taceat sedens,
        Cessabit, ...

    17, 21: <u>vt</u> ... <u>Sic</u> (as a girl charms the senses ... so praise charms the soul).

1563, 1560 and **Autograph:**
    17, 21: <u>non</u> ... <u>Vt</u> (a girl does not charm a youth sc. as much ... as praise charms the soul).

1564, 1560:
    24: <u>Spernit</u> *psallere* (scorns to perform)

1563 and **Autograph:**
    24: <u>Nescit</u> *psallere* (does not know how to perform).

1560:
    16–17: an entire strophe is inserted between these verses:

Artus palladium non oleum fouet
    Defessos, calidi, nec latices, leva‹n›t
    Languentes uigilum, nec
    serus sic oculos sopor
Sensus non iuueni pellicit intimos
    Virgo ...
(Pallas's oil does not so soothe tired limbs
    Nor tepid waters so relieve
    The faint, nor tardy sleep
    So comfort wakeful eyes,
A girl not charm the inmost feelings in
    a youth. ...)

Without the insert, there is sharp, even paradoxical, focus on the sensuous details of the girl's body and gestures: the negative example fascinates and betrays Catullan language and experience. It provoked censorship in another redaction: the bland strophe drives out the piquant (Biblioteca Apostolica Vaticana, *Codices Chigiani Latini*, IV.133, fols. 99–101).

CL IX.12.

Casa claims to have served the Muses from youth to age.

1564:
>si senior tua | nunc uestigia <u>persequor</u>
>(If older now I <u>follow persistently</u> your tracks).

Rome:
>si senior tua | nunc uestigia <u>prosequor</u>
>(If older now I <u>follow in</u> your tracks)

The former more precisely suits the context.

CL IX.29–32.

1564:
>Defensa Hesperia clarus, & <u>impigri</u>
> Compresso celeber militis <u>impetu,</u>
> Bellonae ancipitis <u>numina militis</u>
> Horrere immemoris <u>diu</u>:   32
>(Famed for Italy's defense, renowned because he checked
> the pressing soldier's onslaught, soldier long
> forgetful how to dread
> the powers of shifting war.   32)

Rome:
>Defensa Hesperia clarus, & <u>impetu</u>
> Compresso celeber militis <u>impigri, et</u>
> Bellonae ancipitis <u>mutua numina</u>
> Horrere immemoris <u>ducis</u>:   32
>(Famed for Italy's defense, renowned for onslaught checked
> of soldier never slack and general that
> forgets to dread the treacherous powers
> of War to strike both sides.   32)

The unique witness that Casa composed a book remains the first edition of 1564. The variants confirm what Casa wrote about his penchant for revising: "changing, rechanging and eager to redo yet again, like someone not in a hurry" (*la mia natura è di mutare, e di rimutare, ed ancora di rifar volentieri; come quello, che non ho* [sic] *fretta.*)[109] I have chosen to respect, then, Vettori's 1564 spelling, typography and punctuation, with only an occasional addition or adjustment, which I discuss in the notes. The 1564 edition does not indicate direct address or reported speech, which I do mark to ease reading. Commas often set off themes within larger units, momentarily distracting a reader who expects them to mark logical divsions. In puzzling over these practices, I found that they provoke and repay analysis up to a point. Thus I have preserved the punctuation of the copytext but rarely reported variants in other copies. I have not simply replaced older conventions with modern. I share the opinion "that Renaissance Latin ought to be presented ... in what is undeniably a Renaissance form."[110] Although I can sympathize with the urge for "normalization for the sake of clarity,"[111] I fear that it deprives the reader of an opportunity to engage with a way of reading and interpreting that differs from our own and fluctuates as different interpreters seek to bring out different nuances in a text. As for spelling, few readers will come to Casa's Latin without familiarity with classical texts in modern editions. Such surprises as the inconsistent use of "v/u," for example, may give a flavor of strangeness not irrelevant to entering Casa's cultural world.

---

[109] Casa (Venice) to Vettori, 15 July 1553, *Opere* (1806) 2:175–76.
[110] Fred J. Nichols, ed. and trans., *An Anthology of Neo-Latin Poetry* (New Haven: Yale University Press, 1979), viii.
[111] Paul Oskar Kristeller, "The Editing of Fifteenth-Century Texts. Tasks and Problems," *Italian Culture* 4 (1983): 117.

Giovanni della Casa's Poem Book
Ioannis Casae Carminum Liber

Florence 1564

I

FLAMINII manes, instar mihi numinis vmbra
  Flaminij, hæc campis cernis ab Elysijs?
An tibi, quæ nostri fuerat tam feruida cura,
  Cocytus nigris eluit amnis aquis? 4
Tu solitus Priulique ausus compescere inanes,
  Et molli versus frangere voce truces.
At nunc ille malo Galateum carmine vexat,
  Et sanctum nobis pellit ab vrbe virum. 8
Tu ne ausus, Priuli, Galateum pellere ab vrbe,
  Asperaque in dulcem dicere verba senem?
Tu ne auctor Romæ montani vt munera vici,
  Fumosi vt curam præferat ille laris? 12
Aureus ille senex, vitæ cui licia Parcæ
  Intacta ducunt candidiora niue?
Qui nec Principibus, vrbi nec scilicet ægræ
  Formidet medicas adplicuisse manus? 16
Quemque adeo nemorum custos, pecorisque magister
  Mandarit sacro summus adesse gregi,
Hinc eat, & fuscas ignoti ad flumina Melphæ
  Pascere cum vili coniuge pergat oues? 20
Quid si animis iuuenumque senumque est illius æque
  Dulcior Hybleis alba senecta fauis?
Quid si illum retinent quicumque Amaryllida curant,
  Huius ad exemplum peccet vt illa minus? 24
Vxorem hunc tamen ad vetulamque humilemque releges,
  Frigida vt in viduo ne cubet illa toro?
Quæ puras pridem didicit perducere noctes
  Et monitis casta est & proba facta viri. 28

I

A Country Cure for the Sick City

Flamin's ghost, shade like a god to me
   Of Flamin, from the Elysian fields do you
see this? Or has the gloomy stream of Cocytus
   engulfed your once warm love for us?   4
You used to check Priuli's foolish thrusts,
   You tamed with gentle voice his savage verse.
But now he hurts Galat with wicked song,
   drives from the city one whom we revere.   8
Did you, Priuli, dare to drive him out,
   speak bitter words against a sweet old man,
urge he prefer to Rome these hill-town chores—
   a charge of smoke-grimed country shrines—   12
that golden elder, whose life-threads the Fates
   spin out more white than virgin snow,
who would not fear to lay his healing hands
   on rulers or the city, were it sick,   16
whom even the highest guard of groves, herd master,
   gave command to help his sacred flock?
Should he leave here for unknown Melfi's streams
   to keep black sheep beside a common mate?   20
What if his hoary age to young and old
   seems sweeter than Hyblaean honeycombs?
What if those who guard Amaryllis want him near
   by whose example she might sin the less?   24
Really, would you banish him to a poor old spouse
   so she in a widowed couch does not lie cold?
She long since learned to make the nights pass pure:
   his warnings made her chaste and true.   28

Sed tu Flaminij potius iam nobilis vmbra,
  Et multum insigni conspicienda lyra:
Ni te cæca huius cepere obliuia lucis,
  Cum tibi mors auidas intulit atra manus, 32
Huc ades, & Priulum compescas; nam male nobis
  Iamdudum insolito versus in ore sonat.

II

Vt capta rediens Helene cum coniuge Troia,
Lento homine atque animi lenis, nimiumque remissi,
Incidit in cædem ipsam & funus forte sororis,
Quam præceps miseri virtus iugularat Orestis, 4
Succisam de more comam missura sepulto
Germanæ cineri, fertur dempsisse capillo
Vix tandem e summo paulum, ne forte placeret
Tonsa minus metuens Spartanis improba mœchis: 8
   Haud aliter Galatee malis erroribus actus
Nuper ego, & Phrygios nautas, Paridemque secutus
Aufugi longe: atque idem, rediit tamen vt mens
Ad sese peregre nimium remorata, proteruæ 12
Ornamenta fugæ sensim lenteque repono:
Parui etenim refert Veneris ne cupidine, vt illa,
Incensus, pulchra vel saucius ambitione,
Tramite declinem recto, violemque pudorem. 16
Debueram dudum crinem secuisse decorum:
Hoc est argentum, comites, & stragula, cœnas,
Lususque & musas missas fecisse loquaces,
Intrepidus nuper curatæ mentis & acer 20
Corrector: sed enim prauus populi pudor obstat;
Hunc propter pauidi phaleris amicimur ineptis:
Nec sicci madidam audemus, veriti bene potum
Conuiuam vulgus, collo dempsisse coronam. 24
   Dedecus ambitio pulchrum est, uitiumque fauentis
Laudatum populi studio: I, bone, quo tua uirtus
Te uocat, i pede fausto, et nomen laudibus auge,
Aequales aiunt comitesque piique propinqui: 28
Quod si natura, aut ratio, uirtutis habendos

But rather you, now, shade of Flamin, known
    and much to be noted for your brilliant lyre,
if not cut off and blinded from this light
    since dark death placed its greedy grip on you,   32
come here and check Priuli: troubling us
    too long with altered voice he sounds this verse.

II

The City Blamed for Sickness in the Poet

As Helen, when Troy was taken, coming home
with Menelaus—cold and all too slack—,
arrived at murdered Clytemnestra's rites—
whom rash Orestes' wretched worth had slain—   4
about to pay her sister's ash the curl
required by custom, snipped begrudging, late
and little, just the tip, afraid if shorn
she might have less appeal to Spartan rakes.   8
    Not otherwise did I fly far, Galat,
just now, in foul pursuit of Paris' ilk:
and likewise, as itself my mind comes home
from too long exile, I let go   12
the heady show, but slowly, step-by-step:
slight difference if like her by lust
inflamed or pricked by fine ambition I
desert the right path and dishonor shame.   16
I ought to have cut long since that comely curl—
wealth, I mean, companions, carpets, feasts
and gambling—, rid myself of facile talk,
unflinching, mind new-healed, and keen for right.   20
Yet sleazy shame what folks may think forbids
and makes us wrap ourselves in tasteless show,
nor dare take off the wine-soaked wreath, though sober,
fearing our drunken table-mate, the crowd.   24
    A fine disgrace ambition—vice that's praised
by eager people: "Go where your worth calls you,
Go with luck, and puff your name with praise."
So peers and pals and pious neighbors say.   28
But if nature or reason dictate one must have

Germanas propriasque notas euincat honores,
Publice ut æs signant, extemplo ut noscere, nummus
Quanti quisque siet, possint: per turbida Ponti   32
Curramus rapidi maria, & gelidas properemus
Ipsa hieme in media tantum ad decus ire per alpes,
Obliti podagræ, neruos urentis & artus.
   Nunc prauos inter tituli discrimen inanes,   36
Atque bonos nullum signant: sæpe & toga pectus
Candidius multo, & maius pulla arctaque texit,
Quam laxi, Tyrioque infecti murice amictus:
Nam si legitimum nobis virtutis inurant   40
Fasces & tituli signum; mercetur honores
Ipsa vel vita, informis ne prodeat: inque
Excussus, Priulusque bonus, simplexque Faërnus,
Prudens & veræ virtutis cultor vterque: 44
Vitrea quos numquam titillat gloria, febris
Purgatos huius. Nos quamuis cesserit horror
Atque æstus, sani nondum tamen usque valemus;
Sicque animus positam reminiscitur ambitionem,   48
Vulnus vt obductum prurit tamen, hæret asello
Vt nudo clitellis nonnumquam vlcus in armo.
   Vos agite aureolum tondete a vertice crinem
Lasciuo huic capiti, atque domi cohibete, seueri,   52
Non Menelaus vti, erronem me: tu, Priulusque,
Vtroque & melior Polus (quod dicere vestra
Pace mihi liceat) nitidaque extrudite Roma
Restantem: vt duri mulum quandoque cerebri,   56
Luctantem in triuio, atque equiti parere negantem,
Sibilo agunt primum & magnis clamoribus; inde
Prosiliunt longis armati fustibus: illa
Nixa diu, tandem plagis deterrita currit.   60

III

Si te cura vigil sophiæ delectat: & acre
Ingenium vires si sufficit, utere porro
Munere tam claro diuum: sic rectius atque
Commodius multo, longeque decentius æui   4

worth's badges—true and proper brands,
as men mark bronze to know at once
what each coin weighs—, let's hurry across
the rough Black Sea and run through chilly Alps
in winter's midst to get so great a prize,
forgetting aching legs, sore muscles, gout.
Now empty titles make no sign to mark
depraved from honest: often dingy garb
and tight conceals a cleaner, ampler heart
than do full cloaks with purple dyes.
Suppose that titles, medals did burn in
a legal mark of worth. Why even good
Priuli, frank Faerno would pay life
itself for such, so not to seem formed ill
and ill-alert, though both pursue true worth:
men glassy glory never tickles, free
of fever. We, however much the burning
shakes have passed, are still not wholly well.
My mind keeps bringing up deposed ambition:
likewise healed wounds itch and sores remain
on burros' flanks when packs are taken off.
 You, then, trim at the root the golden curl
from this lewd head and rein me in—unlike
Menelaus—strict when I stray, Priuli, both
you and Pole, our better (let me say),
and drive me forth from glittering Rome,
though I resist like some hard-headed mule
that balks at crossroads, thwarts her rider's will.
They urge at first with shouts and whistling, then
swarm out with long sticks armed: yet she resists
at length, till frightened by the blows she runs.

III

The Healthy Style of Poetic Life

If you delight in wisdom's watchful care,
and keen ability gives strength, enjoy
henceforth the gods' bright gift: thus you will live
more rightly, much more fully, far more fitly

Quod tibi cumque neant Parcæ victurus amicæ.
Nec de te plebis quæ sit sententia, magni
Securus pendas: ignarum pleraque vulgus
Prauo metitur modulo: tu neglige, & isto, 8
Qui nunc te exercet, fugias decedere campo:
An populi arbitrio quisquam plebisque bonorum
Posthabeat sanus plausum, quem iure feres tu:
Quandoquidem cunctos quicumque feruntur eisdem 12
In spatiis, iam recto nimirum ac sapiente
Iudice præcurris Bembo: cum hic interea nos
Desidiæ arguimur populo, ne forte probari
Credideris genus hoc vitæ simplex: etenim ad res 16
Versiculis, missisque iubent accedere nugis:
Ex vmbra & tenebris in solem exire, diemque
Et gnaui me segnem culpant: altera blando
Pars animum integrum queritur me dedere amori 20
Per luxum, & patrui verbis obiurgat acerbi:
Qui simul ac stomachum, quamquam permulta ferenti
Vt placem, morunt: regero grauiora receptis:
Vt proprium seruas auri sceleratus aceruum 24
Vndique congestum: neglectis, iura fidemque
Exponis tota venalem, legibus, vrbe:
Cum miserum atque inopem deiectum rure paterno
Deseris, atque adeo prudens, nummique redemptus 28
Prodis: & emunctum producta lite clientem
Vsque adigis, dum ædes etiam proscribat auitas:
   Turpiter aut vltro seruis, plerumque furentis
Mancipium domini: manibus ten' ferre catinum 32
Cœnanti ingenuis? aliam ten' sumere mentem
Deterioris heri ad nutum atque aliam? haud animo par
Est generi, quicumque suos apud ortus honeste
Imperio abiectus paret trepidusque ministrat. 36
   Quid quod amicitiæ, caro dum cuncta lucello
Metiris, cultus tu nullos, nullaque nosti
Officia: anormique decor concinnus inepto
Quid distet nescis? pecudis næ nos cute tectam 40
Naturam inspicimus, quid publica cum geritur res
Per te, si furtis quo sit locus atque rapinæ,
Bellorum causas iussus præcidere, nutris:
Desidiæ, aut tu me censor culpaueris oti? 44

whatever time your friendly fates spin out.
Nor how the commons view you need you give
great weight, unruffled: much that stupid crowd
weighs basely. Pay no heed, avoid
retreating from the field where you're engaged:
No sane man puts the people's view ahead
of better men's applause, which you will get by right,
since, Bembo, you already far outrun
all others on this course: believe a straight
and canny referee. Yet, meanwhile, we
get charged with sloth by folks, lest you suppose
they prize this simple life. No, they would have
us give up trifling verse for real affairs,
to sunny day from shade and darkness move:
they blame inaction actively, they whine
that we with wheedling love corrupt the pure
in heart; like sour-faced relatives they scold.

 But once they stir my bile, though I for peace
put up with plenty, rougher I retort.
You criminal, you hoard the heap of gold
you got by hook and crook; you break the laws
throughout the city: you put lawful trust on sale.
When you betray the needy wretch that lost
his father's farm, you seem so prudent, hired
for cash. To clean your client out, you stretch
his case till he must sell his forebears' home.

 Or shamefully you often play the slave
to crazy masters, bear with free-born hands
the diner's dish, strike attitudes—now this,
now that—to meet a worse heir's whim, unlike
the honest son-in-law at home who meekly
harks to power and anxiously takes stock.

 And what of friendship, you that measure all
by petty gain, love no one, share no sense
of duty, do not know what's in or out
of place. But we see through your nature camouflaged
in fleece: what if, when government gets run
by you, allowing burglary and theft,
you feed the conflicts you were told to stop,
then you blame me for laziness and sloth?

Flagras ambitione, ardesque cupidine sæua
Purpurei, haud uitam hanc mores ue decentis, amictus.
Vror amoris ego haud me dignis ignibus: esto
Quando ita me insimulas; quid tum? peccamus uterque; 48
Nil est cur tu me prior incuses, grauiora
Offendens multo, & nimium distantia recto:
　　　Nam qui uel paruo conductus peierat, & qui
Tamquam turbata victum sibi quæritat unda 52
Piscator, pacem bellis vbi miscuit, idem,
Iudicium atque crucem si demas, ire latrones
Inter iam uelit & iugulare homines. sua quisque
Defendunt lenes uitia & minuunt; aliena 56
Carpere plerique austeri, nimiumque seueri.
　　　Adde quod incurata gerens, serpentiaque intus
Vlcera corrupto tandem pulmone peribis;
Purgandum illius cum te committere morbi 60
Non medico studeas; annus non vnus & alter
Imminuat quicquam: pulchris macrescere captum
Diuitiis frustra tantum doleamus amici:
Me mea post paulo febrisque reliquerit ultro 64
Frigidior veniens morbum cum leniet ætas,
Intereaque veternus non animum grauis vrget,
Me tamen insequitur populus: quid si nihil omni
Est actum in vita nobis, quod lædere quemquam 68
Possit? non ego rem, mihi sollers quam pater auxit,
In Venerem effundam; neque lite petitus amator
Iniusta, omittam fundumque laremque tueri:
Nec fuerim, mimam quo sit mihi laxius unde 72
Munerer, vsquam inopi nimium contractus amico:
Denique non mos, non ætas alienior: adde,
Ille etiam laqueo statuit qui nectere collum
Auratane trabe, an de putri pendeat ulmo 76
Si quicquam referre putas; quam ego honestius ac tu
Intereo; Seu me Musis & Apolline claro,
Seu quis me pulchro captum culparit amore,
Me tamen insequeris: colloque ac faucibus anguis 80
Inflatis viro vitam deducere inertem
Indignum clamat fucos, segnem malus vrget:
　　　At tecum siquis sic egerit: Itur ad vrbem
Europa ex omni, credo, vt vestigia summo 84

You blaze with pomp and burn with fierce desire
for purple—not this moral life's fit garb.
My fire is love: not worthy, I concede
when you attack. What then? We're sinners both. 48
No reason you accuse me first, since you
offend more gravely, farther from the right.
   For one that perjures, cheaply bribed, and one
that hunts in violent seas for livelihood 52
by fishing, when his wars grow quiet, he,
if made exempt from trial, torture, would
join thieves and cut men's throats: we each defend
our own faults, play them down; it's others' faults 56
we pick at, too censorious and strict.
   Remember that untreated sores will spread
inside, corrupt your lungs, and bring you death.
Unless you place yourself in doctors' care 60
to purge the illness, time alone will not suffice
to cure it: friends would only grieve for you
enthralled by finery, withering away.
My fever will diminish by itself 64
and soon, when cooler years reduce the pain
and stern old age will not stir up the heart.
Yet I get blamed by people. Why, when all
my lifetime nothing that I did could harm 68
another? I'd not spill for love the wealth
my careful father made, nor if unjustly sued
for loving, fail to guard my farm and hearth,
nor ever pledge an actress to a friend 72
too poor to give me back an easy gift—
far from it both in age and style. He's set
to knot his neck a noose: if you suppose
it matters whether from gold or sordid elm 76
he hang, how much more decently than you
I die, if someone fault me as enthralled
by famed Apollo's Muses or fine love.
Yet you chase me. Its maw with venom charged 80
the snake proclaims my life-style loose—
unworthy, drones. Wicked harries slack.
   But one may argue thusly: "City tours
from all of Europe come, I think, to view 84

Inspiciant veteris veneranda in colle Quirini:
Siue in Auentino Romæ. ac non perditus exul
Expes vt quisque est, huc sese contulit, vt si
Bargulum ad Illyricum dicas, latrociniumque   88
Concessum; nimium merito dicatur acerbus.
Oderit & rabidum populusque patresque venenum.
    Non ego: nec vulgi si irritor vocibus hoc nunc
Immeritum quemquam latrarim: possum ego multos   92
Eximere e numero, turpis contagia morbi
Quos nulla attigerint, sanos, recteque valentes:
Sincerum vt Molsæ pectus, lauere salubres
Pierii quem fontis aquæ: puroque Camœnæ   96
Curatum cantu seruant. studioque referti
Spectatus dudum tanto plausuque theatri
Vbaldinus, inops agrique larisque paterni,
Virtutis locuplex. populo spectante Quirini   100
Hunc non donatum scæna decedere turpe est.

IV

In mulieres nuptas Hippolyti. Ex Euripide.

Concinnum in auras luminis hominum malum
Cur protulisse dixerint te feminas
Iuppiter? etenim erat si serendum hominum genus,
Haudquaquam oriri debuit de femina: 4
Sed emere liberorum oportuit sibi
Semina genus mortalium, ferens tua
In templa tantum aut æris, aut auri grauis,
Ferriue, quanti vnus foret quisque pretii,   8
Domosque habere feminis sine liberas.
Nam nunc in ædes vehere cum malum parant,
Extemplo opes pro eo rependunt patrias.
Atque hoc liquet malum esse magnum feminam,   12
Namque ad alienos pellit hanc ex ædibus
A se pater prognatam & eductam, suis,
Additque dotem, vt liberet sese malo:
At ille contra, stirpem in ædes noxiam   16
Qui ad se recepit, lætus est cum pessimam

the awesome relics on old Quirin's hill
or Aventine at Rome. But no poor wretch,
when hopeless, hastens here, as if you'd say
to Balkan Bargul and permitted theft." 88
He justly would be said too harsh.
Both high and low would spurn his venomed rage.
   Not I: nor angered by the crowd would I
unfairly bark at someone. Many I exempt 92
as never touched by contact with the foul
contagion: hale and rightly hearty, like
good Molsa, scrubbed by healthful waters from
Pieria's spring and kept well cured by pure 96
Camenae's song, and likewise Ubaldin,
approved long since by so much eager praise,
packed theaters, poor in family land and home,
yet rich in worth. For him to leave the stage 100
without Quirinus' people's prize is base.

IV

The City Women Blamed
(Of Hippolytus against married women. From Euripides)

Jove, why must they say you brought to light the
well-made ill for humans—woman? If man
had to be created somehow, by no
means should it have been from woman: 4
better if the human race had purchased
seeds of children, placing gold or bronze or
massive iron in shrines of yours, however
great the price for each and every offspring: 8
keeping households wholly free of women.
   Anyone set on bringing home this murrain,
starts by shelling out the family shekels.
That's why woman really greatly troubles, 12
since once born and raised her father drives her
out to strangers, giving her a dowry
just to rid himself of further damage.
But her husband, harboring in his household 16
harmful stock, is happy draping finest

Pulcherrime ornat statuam, & auro & purpura
Certat, beatas sumptibus miser domos
Exhauriens: atque hæret: etenim splendidis 20
Affinibus gauisus vxorem asperam
Perfert: proba at si ea, sed propinqui futiles
Euenerit, bono miseriam comprimit.
Verumtamen commodius euenit, quibus 24
Nullius vxor sedet in ædibus preti,
Ac fatua: nam sapientem ego odi feminam:
Meæ nec intra venerit limen domus,
Quæ, quam mulierem sapere par est, plus sapit: 28
Facilius etenim perspicaces edocet
Astutias, dolosque Cypris improba:
At fatua mulier ob stoliditatem sapit.
Penetrare nempe ad feminas oportuit 32
Nulli licere familiarium, simul
Sed beluarum includere rabiem domi
Loqui insciam, sermonem vt inferre alteri
Ipsa nequirent, nec alii illas adloqui: 36
Nunc facinora, intus quæ malæ mala cogitant
Dominæ, foras hæc familiares efferunt.

V

Cum ab Vrbe profectus, Venetias iret

HVmida Tyrrheni fugientem flamina venti
 Cælumque pestilens Lati,
Me Venetum excipient mitissima littora, & auræ
 Salubriores, putribus 4
Iam membris senio, & podagra turgentibus acri;
 Quæ flare suerunt nec mala
Imbutæ tussi, neque in ipsis fluctibus udæ
 Faerne, mireris licet: 8
Prorsus, qui Romam liquit, rerum ille carebit
 Pulcherrimo spectaculo;
Nec cœtum æque illustrem hominum, nec Palladis æque
 Instructa pectora artibus, 12

goods on worst of busts: he vies with gold and
purple—wretch, with spending empties out his
happy home—and keeps on, since he likes her 20
rich relations, bearing with a bitter
wife; or if she's good, but her family's no-good,
she subdues their poorness with his riches.
   All in all it proves more advantageous 24
just to get a wife of no great value,
simple, too: I hate a clever woman:
not across the threshold of my dwelling
let a woman come more clever than she 28
should be: since too easily wicked Cypris
teaches tricks and penetrating dodges.
Simple women get good sense from dullness.
Surely access to the women's quarters 32
should not ever be permitted servants:
better bring home angry beasts that don't know
how to speak, can't carry out to others
gossip or be gossiped to by others. 36
Now whatever trouble tricky housewives
plot inside, gets told by servants outside.

V

To Flee the City for a Cure
(When setting out from Rome to go to Venice)

When I escape the humid blasts of Tuscan winds
   and Latium's sickly sky,
Venetians' very gentle shores and healthier breeze
   will welcome me—though weak 4
my limbs by now with age and swollen with sharp gout—
   light breezes not imbued
with hacking coughs and not, though over waters, damp:
   Faerno be amazed! 8
No doubt one leaving Rome is going to miss the great
   substantial spectacle:
no throngs of men as brilliant and no heads
   as stocked with Pallas' arts 12

Terrarum ut cunctas lustret circumuagus oras,
  Offendet vsquam gentium;
Fragmina nec muri aspiciet maiora uetusti
  Non diminutis urbibus; 16
In primis Bromij latices & frigida siccis
  Requiret idem faucibus
Pocula lympharum sub terras condita opacas,
  Aut fossa Lucanam in niuem: 20
Ipse ego, feruenti delapsam ex imbrice lympham
  Nuper, nec altos in scrobes,
Et uappam, salices inter quæ nata palustres
  Cæni saporem patrij 24
Potanti offundet, mediis feruoribus, ardens
  Arente fauce traxero:
Ast idem hospitibus placidos & dulcia pacis
  Impertientes commoda 28
Mortales cernam, & locupletem ciuibus vrbem
  Dispar probantibus nihil:
Cernam loricam uiolentam, ensemque superbum
  Inermibus suffragijs 32
Constrictum, & diræ execratum cædis amorem
  Longe exulantem gentium:
Illic cum cano prudentia sera capillo
  Paret uicissim, & imperat: 36
Illo se nusquam propendens contulit æquum
  Bonæ comes concordiæ,
Fraudibus Hesperia vt pulsum est, timuitque rapacis
  Vncas licentiæ manus. 40

VI

De Vbaldino Bandinellio

TAM caro capiti iam nimium diu
  Munus Melpomene lugubre, Næniam
  Debemus: querulam prome puer lyram.
    Siccis non ego te genis, 4
Mœrore aut vacuus pectora lurido
  Laudabo: neque desiderium moræ

will he engage: not though scouring every strand
    of land and every folk.
No greater breaks in ancient wall will he observe,
    unless in towns destroyed.   16
Right off with thirsty throat will he regret the flow
    of gurgling wine and cups
of chilly waters stored beneath dark earth or dug
    inside Lucanian snow: 20
Myself, on fire, throat dry with summer heat, will draw
    a draft of water dripped
just then from sun-warmed gutters, hardly deep in wells,
    insipid stuff, like that   24
which, brought from marshes green with willows, gives the cup
    a taste of homegrown muck.
But all the same I will discern men kind to guests
    imparting sweet rewards   28
of peace: a city rich in citizens inclined
    to nothing out of plumb.
I will discern the violent breastplate and proud sword
    by votes and not by force   32
constrained, and hateful love of dreadful butchery
    to distant exile sent.
In that place Foresight late in life her hair grown white
    obeys and rules by turns: 36
there Justice, never predisposing, found a home,
    good comrade of accord,
when driven from the West by fraud and fearing hooks
    of misrule's grasping hands.   40

VI

Honoring a Florentine Master's Gifts
(On Ubaldino Bandinelli)

To one so dear we owe already now
too long, Melpomene, the grieving gift
of threnody. Get out the plaintive lyre.
    With cheeks not dry   4
I'll praise you, since my heart is not yet free
of pallid mourning: neither tardiness

         Nostrum diminuunt, aut hominum atterens
         Furtim tristitiam dies.   8
Te morum studium, te sapientiæ
         Cura, & nobilium fecerat artium
         Vbaldine quies gnaua, operosaque
         Musarum otia diuitem,   12
Non auri, pauidis addere mentibus
         Mordacem validi sollicitudinem,
         Non ostri, experiens quod reparat Ligur
         Nobis merce superflua: 16
Irrite, fugiens pauperiem, æquora
         Iracunda leui nauita palmula;
         Aestatem Libyæ perferat igneam
         Idem, idem Aemonias niues,   20
Vestigans lapides, femina quos petit
         Vel flauo capiti, vel tereti decus
         Collo. Mentibus Atlantiades Deus
         Calcar subdere inertibus   24
Ludens dum cuperet, fertur inutile
         Promsisse aurum, acuens illo hebetes, uti
         Exercet puerum non vegetum nuce
         Mater sedula futili: 28
At fortes (quoniam robore stat suo
         Virtus, Peliaca vt quercus, & æquoris
         Saxum Carpathij) nec famulæ decet
         Auscultare pecuniæ,   32
Nec firmos fragili fidere: defluit
         Fortuna, vt subitis auctior imbribus
         Extemplo aret aquæ riuus inops suæ,
         Nimbos si pepulit Deus.   36
Tu dulcem es Latij copiam adeptus, &
         Graium diuitias, & dominam vrbium
         Artem: quo mihi nunc & patriæ occidis
         Multo flebilior tuæ: 40
Arni moeret enim fluminis accola,
         Florens ingenijs accola fluminis
         Arni, tot te animi compositis diu
         Thesauris, tacitum mori: 44
Vt nauim pelago præcipitans notus
         Vertit; quæ remorans, largiter alueum

nor stealthy time that dulls grief's edge
    cuts our desire. 8
Your bent for morals, care for wisdom, calm
intensity in famous arts, repose
that kept the Muse employed made you,
    Ubaldin, rich, 12
Not gold, that adds a gnawing anxiousness
to minds already undermined by fear,
not purple dye the canny Genovese
    trades overpriced. 16
The sailor fleeing poverty would prick
the sea to wrathfulness with nimble oars,
would stand the fiery Libyan summer heat
    and Balkan snows 20
to hunt out stones that women want
to deck an auburn head or well-turned throat.
To set a spur to sluggish human minds,
    the god of commerce, 24
Mercury, for sport, they say, doled out
the useless gold to hone dull wits: as when
a tireless mother teases backward boys
    with no-good shells. 28
The strong, however, since worth stands through its
own strength, like mountain oak in Greece or some
Aegean island rock, need not pay heed
    to servile coin 32
nor, firm, put trust in frail. Quick down the drain
goes fortune, just as when a gulley filled
with sudden rains goes dry as soon as Jove
    dispels the clouds. 36
The sweet supplies of Latium you obtained
and wealth of Greeks and art that governs cities:
hence the more your death brings tears to me
    and yours at home: 40
for she who dwells by river Arno mourns—
in flower with genius dwells by Arno's stream—
that you who gathered treasure-troves of mind
    in silence died: 44
as when a wind strikes sudden, fierce, and whips
a ship about that for return had stuffed

Implerat spatiosum: illa Arabum ferens
    Gazas, illa ebur Indicum,   48
Et gratum redolens thus superis ferens,
    Et pexa e folijs vellera sericis,
    Aetnææ Cereris plenaque frugibus,
    Portus strenua patrios   52
Ditaret, populos & procul oppidis
    Effusos studio ad se raperet lucri:
    Nunc sæui arbitrio voluitur Adriæ
    Cæcis obruta fluctibus.   56
At tu, progenies aurea fulmine
    Gaudentis Iouis, o desere ne meum
    Carmen, Musa: diu sed vigeat sacri
    Custos pagina nominis.   60
Hic me Castalij tramitis arduos
    Flexus, Aeoliæ hic me docuit Lyræ
    Ictus; O nebulam obliuio & arceat
    Furuam a nomine splendido   64
Noctem: ne volucris filia temporis
    Ne rubiginis atræ admoueas meis
    Dentem carminibus, neu nigra nubibus
    Condas Italiæ decus.   68

VII

Ad Hannibalem Oricellarium nepotem.
diligentissime cauendum esse ab adulatoribus.

MEntem blandiciæ perdere credulam
    Norunt non secus, ac mortiferas malæ
    Multo melle nouercæ
    Olim cum medicant dapes.   4
Viro imbuta malo dulcia murmura
    Mendacis fuge linguæ, et teneras neque
    Falsis laudibus aures
    Admoris, cupidus puer   8
Verarum, bona ni decipit indoles;
    Et tete excutias, tinniet improba
    Nugas cum modulans uox;
    Quas atro rapidi ferent   12

its ample hold with Arab booty or
    with Indic tusk, 48
transporting incense pleasing to the gods
and fleeces combed from China's leaves of silk
and heaping harvests of Sicilian grain,
    restless to make 52
its home port rich and plunder for itself—
hell-bent on gain—the peoples of far towns,
yet now whipped back at Adriatic's whim
    and blindly drowned. 56
But you, o golden child of Jove who takes
delight in thunder, o, do not desert
my song, Muse: long be strong the page that guards
    his awesome name. 60
He taught the winding, steep Castalian path
to me, he taught me how to pluck the beat
of lyric: let no fog forgetful dim
    his shining name, 64
no swarthy night: the daughter of swift time
should not apply the tooth of gloomy rust
to songs of mine nor, dark with clouds, put down
    Italy's pride. 68

VII

Warning against Sly Flattery
(To Annibale Rucellai his nephew)

Flattery can ruin trustful minds,
no otherwise than stepmothers once masked
    in copious honey
    dishes laced with death. 4
Sweet sounds with vicious venom drenched
of tricky talk abhore; your tender ears
    don't bend to pandering
    praises, child, in place 8
of truth (if your good nature doesn't dupe).
Just shake yourself awake when wicked tongues
    enticing ring out
    trifles that swift winds 12

Cum fumo Boreæ & puluere sordido:
    Ni quicumque libens dicier audies
    Verbis, te labor illum
    Rebus finxerit arduus.   16
Sensus ut iuueni pellicit intimos
    Virgo candida, cum turgidulas tegens
    Nulla ueste papillas
    Molli illum recipit sinu,   20
Sic laudes animum, uera ubi concinunt,
    Permulcere solent: nec mulier tamen
    Vt cantu sine dulcis
    spernit psallere tibiæ,   24
Sic virtus, populus si taceat sedens,
    Cessabit: nihilo nec minus obsita
    Noctis ferueat umbra
    Et deserta silentio   28
Quam cum per medias inclita ducitur
    Vrbes, & celebris uoce fauentium
    Direpta hostibus arma
    Affigit foribus deûm.   32
Cum laudis faciem sumpserit impudens
    Fraus, affinxerit & cum tibi non tua
    Blanda nomina voce
    Et dulcem illecebram struet,   36
Ne te præcipitem trudat amor tui,
    Ne nugis capiare, ut uolucris solet
    Dulci paruula cantu
    Tecti uepribus aucupis.   40

VIII

Ad Fortunam

Expers consilij, quæ pede lubrico
Incedis, zephyris mobilior Dea
Et fluctu Ionij incertior æquoris;
Te, cum læta sinum pandis, & vberes   4
Fundis diuitias, ac miseris ades
Improuisa, boni progeniem Iouis

will snatch with smoke and grimy dust: unless,
whoever you will willingly be called
   in words, in fact hard
   work has made you him.   16
Compare a young man's inward feelings when
a gleaming girl without a dress to hide
   her stiffening nipples
   draws him to her lap: 20
so praises coax the mind, when even truths
they swell. But not, then, like a woman who
   disdains to sing with-
   out a sweet flute's lure,   24
must worth, if people fail to praise, sit back,
or be less fervid, even when oppressed
   by shade of night in
   silence left alone   28
than when led forth in triumph through the midst
of cities, hymned by favoring folk, to nail
   on gods' doors trophies
   seized from hostile arms.   32
When impudent deceit puts on the mask
of praise and uses wheedling speech to make
   you names not yours and
   set inveigling snares,   36
don't let self-love push you over, don't get caught
by trifles, like a little bird by song
   alluring where a
   trapper lurks in briars.   40

VIII

Warning against Shifty Fortune
(To fortune)

Devoid of purpose, Fortune, you step out
with slippery foot, more shifty than the breeze,
and more unsettled than the flux of waves.
When you are glad and pour with open lap   4
abundant wealth and visit poor men's homes
unheralded, they call you child of goodly

Dicunt. Tu ratio, tu sapientia,
Seruatrix eadem crederis vrbium, 8
Virtutisque sedens in solio nites;
Sed mox torua domos regum ubi concutis,
Et congesta diu munera, turribus
Deiectis, subito turbine dissipas, 12
Vanæ te comitem stultitiæ ferunt
Deliram; Immeritum tu, titulo bonis
Dempto, nobilitas; frena superbiæ
Atris tu manibus detrahis ebriæ 16
Successu, & ruere hanc sic temere ad suum
Rides arbitrium, mox humilem truces
Vultus deposituram: O utinam meæ
Oblita ostiolum prætereas domus, 20
Seu tu sanguineis oppida territans
Bellis, ingrederis per Latium fera,
Seu pacemque gerens, & populos beans
Pennis inuolitas uersicoloribus: 24
Nam sic instabilem uisere te meos,
Vel lætam atque hilarem, pertimeam lares.

IX

De Francisco Tornuno Cardinali

QVO tollor pauidus? quo feror insolens?
   O quæ Castalijs fontibus aureos
   Crines, osque lauis virgineum, genus
     Magni Melpomene Iouis, 4
Cruri purpureos indue candido
   Soccos: nam iuga transmittimus alpium
   Soli: unus enim est mi comes argui
     Mendaci metuens pudor: 8
Vatem diua tuum tu moneas uiæ:
   Si pure colui uestra puer sacra
   Feruens mente noua, si senior tua
     Nunc uestigia persequor 12
Quercus umbriferas inter & ilices
   Quærens aërias. Non ego diuitum

Jove, believe that you are reason, you
are wisdom, you the cities' guarantor:
enshrined upon the throne of worth you shine.
But soon when grim you shake the homes of kings
and sudden in a whirlwind scatter years'
accumulated wealth and throw down towers,
then deviant they call you, traveling mate
of folly: fame you give where undeserved,
remove good name from good, withdraw with your
dark hands the bar to drunken pride's
advance, and laugh that by her own free will
she rashly tumbles, soon to put behind
her haughty glances, humbled. O may you,
forgetful of my house, go past my little
door, if savagely you march through Latium
terrifying towns with bloody wars,
or waging peace and making peoples rich
you fly on wings forever changing hues:
for so unstable, even when you're bright
and glad, I'd fear to have you call at home.

IX

Praising the Healer of the West
(On Francis Cardinal De Tournon)

Where am I lofted, awed and strangely stirred?
O you who use Castalia's springs to cleanse
your golden hair and maiden face, O kin
    of mighty Jove,
Put purple boots on your white limbs: for we,
Melpomene, will cross the Alps, our one
companion Modesty that shies from any
    truck with lies.
Your bard remind, o Goddess, of the way:
if ever I in boyhood kept your rites
with pure, new mind, if older now I still
    seek out your tracks
pursuing you through lofty ilex groves
and shady oaks. I never learned to make

  Vanis edidici perstrepere auribus
   Empto carmine: non ego   16
Corruptus pretio nunc meditor parum
  Castæ ducere te ad uestibulum domus.
  At tu prome puer, prome age barbiton
   Cessantem nimium diu.   20
Spartanus ueluti, per nemus asperum
  Dumis insidiantem ut pecori lupum
  Egit, cum fremitu & laude fauentium
   Pagorum redit ad gregem,   24
Villorumque globos sanguine sordidos
  Fert rictu generoso, e iugulis feri
  Vulsos hostis, aquas sic repetit sui
   Tornunus Rhodani, bene   28
Defensa Hesperia clarus, & impigri
  Compresso celeber militis impetu,
  Bellonæ ancipitis numina militis
   Horrere immemoris diu: 32
Alternæ sedenim ille admonuit ferum
  Fortunæ, celeri uertere turbine
  Gaudentis uacuum corpus, vti choros
   Lasciuæ iuuenes ubi   36
Ducunt, &, Zephyris huc agitantibus
  Atque illuc, Phrygio Sidonias acu
  Illusas chlamydes, instabili citæ
   Lustrant atria poplite.   40
Directa ingrediens passibus æquitas
  Ad normam paribus, nec modulo sibi
  Maiore, atque alijs commoda diuidens,
   Quorum non dubia est comes,   44
Illos ære micans non peditum cohors,
  Non sæuis equitum turma frementium
  Horrens cuspidibus terreat, aut mari
   Vectæ cæruleo rates: 48
Nam recto fauet, & iustitiam bono
  Plerumque æquus alit Iuppiter exitu,
  Obscuram & tonitru, & fulmine territans
   Fraudem, atque implicitos dolos   52
Nudans. At uigilem fallit amabilis
  Acrem simplicitas, & super æneas

for rich men's empty ears commotion bought
    as song. Nor do 16
I now, corrupted for a price, have any mind
to take you to a place not chaste enough.
But now bring out, bring out, I say, the lyre
    too long withheld. 20
A Spartan that, in woodlands rough with briars,
has driven off a wolf that ambushed sheep
to shouts and praise of cheering countrymen
    rejoins his herd 24
and grinning broadly brings the globs of wool
he tore all stained with blood from hostile teeth
and jaws: so Tournon to his native Rhone
    returns with fame, 28
the West made safe, renowned because he checked
the pressing soldier's onslaught, soldier long
forgetful how to dread
    the powers of shifting war. 32
Those savages he warned against the whim
of Fortune, how she takes delight to twirl
in whirlwinds idle bodies, like the dance
    licentious girls 36
conduct and dart with limber knees about
grave halls, while breezes toss and swirl, now here,
now there, Phoenician cloaks embroidered with
    a Phrygian point. 40
Straight instead with steps that toe the mark
treads Fairness, portioning herself a part
no greater; no, she shares her goods with others,
    their sure friend: 44
they need not fear foot-soldiers' flashing bronze
or gnashing horsemen's troop that bristles dense
with savage spears or raiders sent to scour
    the sky-blue sea; 48
for Fairness favors right and fairly Jove
most often nurtures Justice with success,
his bolts of thunder striking fear to fraud
    and stripping bare 52
concealed deceits. But dear Simplicity
outsmarts dyspeptic doubt, and over gates

>   Accersita fores, & super ardua
>   Pernix mœnia transilit. 56
> Hanc puro retinens in gremio fouet,
>   Sincere Italiam & diligit hospitam
>   Tornunus, patriam ciuis uti suam,
>   Natorum, & memor aureæ 60
> Ciuis coniugis: hunc purpureus pudor,
>   Elutisque fides candida sordibus,
>   Et presso digitis ore silentium
>   Arcanum insequitur, neque 64
> Infandumque nefas ense domans Themis
>   Districto comitem se negat inclyto
>   Impolluta seni, mundaue ueritas
>   Albo lucida pallio. 68
> Ergo permadidos felle animos nigro
>   Regum, diluere est ausus, & asperæ
>   Permulcere manu pectora turbidæ
>   Plena iræ, intrepidam struens 72
> Pacem, quæ manibus sanguineis diu
>   Attrectata, magis post niteat, uelut
>   Fulgentes lapides, æraue lucida
>   Cum tergere uolunt, luto 76
> Conspurcant: id agens egregius senex
>   Celtarum procerum sanguis, & oppida
>   Firmans obtinuit Marte labantia
>   Quassante, & miseris suas 80
> Vrbes restituit ciuibus, impigram
>   Pacem, tela cruenta inter & asperos
>   Procudens sonitus ferri: etenim gelu
>   Torpens quam peperit timor 84
> Pacem; seruiet illa, horrisoni simul
>   Bellonæ strepitus ingruerint feræ,
>   Imbellis. sedenim desine feruidos
>   Dulcis Melpomene modos: 88
> Nam nec cuncta pudor fert, neque ueritas
>   Cum lucro alma decorum explicuit caput
>   Semper: tum melius tecta silentio
>   Virtus inuidiam latet. 92

of brass, when called, and bastions high
    she nimbly leaps. 56
Now Tournon fondles her in his pure lap
and frankly loves his hostess, Italy,
as citizens love homeland, citizens
    in mind of sons 60
and golden consorts: blushing Modesty
and candid Trust, cleansed pure of filth,
and secret Silence—lips with fingers pressed—
    escort Tournon. 64
Not stainless Law that tames unblushing crime
with naked sword nor Truth, well-scrubbed, white-shirted,
beaming, shirks the brilliant oldster's boon
    companionship. 68
Therefore the anger drunken with black gall
of kings he dared dissolve and, soothing, stroke
by hand hearts filled with rough, roiled wrath, intent
    on lifting fear 72
so Peace, manhandled long by bloody hands,
might shine more brightly after: just as when
they want to burnish brass or polish stone
    to shine, they smear 76
it first with mud: so doing, grand old man
of Celtic princes' blood, he saved and steadied
towns collapsed by shocks of war and gave
    their cities back 80
to wretched citizens, a not slack peace
he hammered out amidst the clang of iron
and gory weapons: for in truth, a peace
    that gelid fear 84
immobile brings to birth will bend enslaved,
without defense, as soon as war's grim noise
bears down. But now withdraw, Melpomene,
    the fevered sounds. 88
For neither modesty tells all nor truth
with profit always bares it's proper head:
then better under shield of silence hides
    from envy worth. 92

X

SVnt qui versiculo minutiore,
Verum pernitido atque perfluenti
Tamquam palladij liquore oliui,
Complures properent linire chartas; 4
Atque, araneoli angulos domorum
Vt tela tenui solent replere
Quantumuis facile, ore fila paruo
Nentes longa, ita compleant libellos 8
Totos uersiculo minutiore:
Hi vatum in numero an ne sint habendi
Vulgus viderit, atque siqua uulgo
Pars vatum est similis, quibus Thalia 12
Flacci sordeat, optimi poetæ,
Quod is uersiculo minutiore
Atque perfacili atque perfluenti
Totas spreuerit occupare chartas. 16

XI

De Margarita regis Gallorum sorore.

Hev mos, vt atris sæpe coloribus
    Contaminatus purum animum inquinas
    Vix eluendis sordibus per
        Tædia solliciti laboris: 4
Me vitreis & fontibus & coma
    Siluæ virentis lætum, & amabile
    Ruris silentium sequentem
        Aoniæ puerum Camœnæ 8
Mersere sacri gurgite fluminis,
    Intacta ut essem candidior niue:
    Immunda sed mox polluit me
        Roma luto nimium tenaci, 12
Quod longa nec dum discutiat dies,
    Sacri nec amnes hactenus abluant;

X
A Brief for Brevity in the Book

Some with verselet rather slender,
but quite fluent and quite sparkling
like the drops from Pallas' olive,
eager smear great lots of pages: 4
like the spiders filling houses'
crannies easy as you please with
wispy weaving—tiny mouths that
spin long threads—so these fill booklets   8
whole with verselet rather slender.
If among the bards they number,
let the crowd see, and such bards as
with the crowd consider poorly   12
Flaccus' muse, though best of poets,
since with verselet rather slender
and quite easy and quite sparkling
he disdained to claim whole pages.   16

XI
Honoring a Princess, Blaming Himself
(On Margaret the French King's sister)

Habit, how, when mixed with muddy pigments,
you pollute the stainless mind, ingraining
    spots not easily dissolved by
    even tiring, anxious work.   4
Taking joy in glass-clear springs and grass-green
woodland shade, desiring country-lovely
    quiet, long ago in boyhood
    my Italian muses dipped   8
me in sacred pools to make me
gleam more white than virgin snow, but all too
    soon then filthy Rome stepped in to
    sully me with sticky mud,   12
which unhurried time would not yet scatter,
hallowed rivers not yet cleanse. Instead my

>   Quin horret & me, & ora cæno
>   Fœda nigro refugit Thalia. 16
> Vulgus venenis vertere Colchicis
>   Plerasque mentes aptius, eripit
>   Sensus priores, atque mutat
>   Alba nigris, maculisque gaudet: 20
> Impurus atra quem populus manu
>   Tractarit, ille & decolor & niger
>   Erit diu, obductamque fæcem
>   Vix iterans remouebit annus, 24
> Notam relinquens: at mihi candidæ
>   Mandanda uirgo est regia paginæ
>   Farnesio iubente, bacca
>   Purius illa nitens Eoa, 28
> Intaminato digna cani, deæ,
>   Est ore, lucis Castalijs deæ
>   Quæ vulgus arcetis profanum,
>   Et nitido prohibetis amne, 32
> O tetra tandem consilia hæc bonæ
>   Obliuioni tradite turbidæ;
>   Labemque nobis rore sacro
>   Abluite, illuuiemque vulgi. 36

XII

Deflet mortem Horatij Farnesij.

> TE flebimus flos Hesperiæ puer
>   Madente multis carmine lacrimis;
>   Et, debitam laudi Thaliam,
>   Nænia lugubris occupabit: 4
> Ille, ense pectus qui tibi candidum
>   Traiecit, ijsdem uulneribus Lati
>   Cecidit & spes, & uirescens
>   Italiæ decus ense carpsit, 8
> Horati, eodem. Non ego sauciam
>   Ictu parentem mortifero tuam
>   In lacrimas culpem ruentem,
>   Nec uiduæ gemitus puellæ 12

Muse with shudders shrinks and flees my
　　lips still foul with blackened muck. 16
Vulgar people, often apt to turn our
heads with sly seductions, steal our erstwhile
　　moral sense, switch black for white, and
　　take delight in spreading spots. 20
One the dirty crowd with grimy hands has
clapper-clawed will long remain discolored—
　　black: a year returning hardly serves to
　　wipe away the filthy smear, 24
still unclean. But my white page is meant to
be entrusted with a princess royal,
　　by Farnese's wish: the girl, more
　　shining pure than eastern pearl, 28
merits praises sung by never sullied
lips, o goddesses, who shut Castalia's
　　groves against the crowd outside and
　　keep reserved the sparkling stream. 32
Really, goddesses, be good, and hand these
gloomy counsels off to dim forgetting:
　　wash away with hallowed dew our
　　stain and soiling by the crowd. 36

XII

Consoling a Princess, Praising a Hero
(He mourns the death of Horace Farnese)

You, the West's young flower, we mourn for,
pouring song that flows with copious weeping:
　　grieving threnody preempts my
　　Muse from praises owed before. 4
He who drove the swordthrust through your pure white
breast with those same wounds cut down for Latium
　　hopes and plucked by that same swordthrust
　　Italy's honor growing green, 8
Horace. Nor would I lay blame against your
mother, injured by the deadly impact,
　　breaking down with strong lamenting;
　　nor your new girl-widow's groans 12

Compescere ausim carmine: lugeat
  Immo illa dulces funere nuptias
  Miscens amaro, nec sat umquam
  Te misera illacrimata flerit: 16
Iam nec capillo parcere, nec genis
  Aequum puella est regia, lacrimis
  Efflagita Martem cruentum
  Vberibus, pueri cadentis 20
Dulces ocellos, & tua gaudia,
  Quæ conciderunt exorientia:
  Vt stella, quæ uix dum coorta
  Hesperium occulitur sub æquor. 24
Non ille auorum, nec soceri immemor:
  Dulcique flagrans igne tui, neci
  Vltro obuios gressus superbos
  Intulit, intrepidumque pectus 28
Obiecit hosti, qua uiolentius
  Bellona nigris fœda cruoribus
  Est uisa Martis sæuientis
  Sanguineas glomerare turmas. 32
Nunc lætus umbras uulnera nobiles
  Ostentat inter pulchra, nemus tenens
  Beatum, ubi Hectorque & Latini
  Sunt ueteres, Rutulique Reges: 36
At Thespijs o grata sororibus
  Obliuiosi pellere temporis
  Idonea umbram, atræque mortis,
  Gloria, vulneribus mederi; 40
O trade Musis & Polyhymniæ
  Custodiendum nomen Horatij
  Clarum, & domum Farnesiorum
  Hanc Latij, Italiæque lumen. 44

would I dare reproach in verses: rather, let her
give herself to grief and temper marriage
 sweets with bitter dirges, poor child,
  never mourning you enough.   16
Not now, royal girl, the time to
leave your hair and cheeks untorn, while calling
 back from killer Mars with flooding
  tears your fallen husband-boy's   20
charming eyes and your enjoyments, which have
perished just as they were first beginning
 like a star that barely risen
  sets beneath the western sea.   24
Not forgetting forebears nor your kingly
father, sweetly fired by you, he freely
 brought his haughty stride to meet with
  murder and his fearless heart   28
threw against the foe, where fiercely brutal
Battle, fouled in clotted blackness, took her
 stand to heap up helter-skelter
  raging Mars's bloody troops.   32
Happy now he makes display of handsome
wounds to noble ghosts, frequenting blessed
 groves with ancient heroes—Hector,
  Latin and Italian kings.   36
Glory, o beloved by Grecian muses,
gifted in the art of exorcising
 time's forgetful shadow and of
  treating wounds from gloomy death,   40
may you to muses hymning many praises
hand along the name to keep it famous:
 Horace and Farnese family,
  Italy's and Latium's light.   44

XIII

In Petrum Victorium.

NObis Calliope magnum alienum æs superest uetus:
Nam pridem ratio scripta mihi est pectore in intimo:
Tu quæso patere a te soluam quidquid id est dea.
Non Victorius est exiguis uersibus, aut lyræ   4
Aptandus tenui: vester amat Phœbus eum, neque
Vlli plura bonum munifica crediderim manu
Largitum: uber enim sicut ager, ruraque pampino
Mitis florida Iacchi, & Bromio & frugibus oppida   8
Circum plena hilarant, muneribus diues Apollinis
Etruscos populos ingenij fruge bona bonus
Ille enutrit alens. Sic senior uertice Pelij
Olim Phyllirides frondifero semifer uberi   12
Graios nobilium seminio dicitur artium
Ditasse. Ille dies e medio tollere qui potest
Ritu Cecropio scripta tibi clara volumina,
Victori, eripiet roriferis sidera noctibus,   16
Idem subtrahet & piscibus, idem æquora nantibus.
Contages populi te tetigit lurida morbidi
Numquam, te ambitio curriculum prætereuntium
Obliquis oculis aspiciens nec pepulit, neque   20
Illi roboris hoc attribuit Iuppiter, ut sacrum
Phœbo discutiens commoueat pectus, originem
A Cœo licet, & Porphyrione a ualido trahat
Conatis solium Cælicolum scandere fratribus.   24
Non res, cui cumulus semper abest, cuncta ue metiens
Aurum te pupugit: te nitidum Musa salubribus
Fontis Castalij lauit aquis candida, tu meæ
Es lumen patriæ percelebris: sat mihi fructuum   28
Ignaua hæc tulerint exilia in montibus asperis
Quæsita, argueris desidiæ ni tibi debitum
Carmen, ni ue inopis quod citharæ dinumerem modos,
acceptum id mihi te ferre neges, iureque respuas.   32

XIII

Praising a Florentine Master's Gifts
(On Pier Vettori)

A great and long-outstanding debt, Calliope, we owe:
the promissory note was written early in my heart.
I beg you, goddess, let me pay through you the full amount.
Victorius cannot be quit with penny-pinching verse   4
and stingy lyre: your Phoebus values him too dear, on him,
and no one else, I think, has lavished greater good, with hand
more large: consider fertile farmland, countryside that brims
with tender shoots of gentle Bacchus, how with Bromius and fruits 8
it fills and cheers surrounding towns: so he, enriched with gifts
Apollo gave, enriches, good with goodly fruit of talent feeds
the Tuscan peoples. So an elder once upon a time
on Pelion's leafy peak, the centaur, Chiron, Phylliris' son,   12
half-beast, the story goes, with fertile breed of noble arts
made rich the Greeks. That day which can remove from us the famous
books that you, Victorius, wrote with ancient Grecian style,
that day will likewise steal away the stars from dewy night,   16
and that same day withdraw the sea from swimmers and from fish.
The sickly people's sallow-faced contagion never got
to you: ambition that with sidelong glances eyes the rush
of passing runners never did unhinge you, nor did it   20
from Jove obtain enough of oaklike strength to force retreat
and bring to nought the awesome heart of Phoebus, even though
ambition traces back its roots to brother giants—Ceus
and brute Porphyrion—that tried to scale the sky gods' throne.   24
Not greed that never runs a surplus, nor gold out-weighing all,
has ever stung you. You, the pure white Muse washed sparkling clean
with healthful waters of Castalia's spring, o light of my
much celebrated fatherland: enough for me the yield   28
that will have been engendered by this lazy exile sought
amidst harsh hills, unless you fault for indolence this song
in debt, or, what I pay in measures of a meager lyre
that I accredit, you discount and, in your rights, reject.   32

XIV

O quæ terrificos vicina e turre cietis
  Tot nocte æra sonos tinnula, totque die;
Si mihi uenturæ noctis dormire licebit
  Per tot tinnitus particulam misero,   4
Nec cum defessos iam iam continget ocellos,
  Vos metuet subito, diffugietque sopor,
Ipse ego cras vobis vltro tortique rudentis
  Spiras, & firmo e robore fulcra dabo;   8
Tutius ut sonitu boreamque lacessere sæuo
  Possitis posthac, & maria, & tonitrus.

XV

Cum cinctum nimbis et nigra nube sedentem
  Deficient olim flammea tela Iouem:
Cum sueta in pontum plenis decurrere ripis
  Præcipitem sistent flumina prona pedem: 4
Fluctibus & raucis Siculum pertundere littus
  Ionij cum iam desinat unda maris:
Tunc quoque uicinis suspensa in turribus æra
  Cessabunt bombos edere raucisonos.   8

XVI

Cum mare nec fremitus edet, nec sibila venti,
  Nec nimbi, abruptis nubibus igne, sonum:
Et cum nubigenæ Thaumantidis ora sinumque
  Deficiet croceus, purpureusque color: 4
Cum pontum nitidi pisces, cum littora pictæ
  Conchæ, cum densum deseret umbra nemus:
Turre tua tunc, Corneli dulcissime, raucos
  Tinnula cessabunt æra ciere sonos.   8

No Cure for a Country Ill

XIV

You brassy bells that from the neighbor belfry belt
   out frightful noises both by day and night,
if just a little bit of this next night for sleep
   you might allow me—suffering from your sounds—,
if slumber, just about to touch my worn out eyes,
   does not take sudden fright of you and flee,
I freely promise I'll donate tomorrow new coils
   of twisted hemp and props of solid oak
so your fierce noise more soundly after this
   can challenge thunder, sea, and northern blasts.

XV

At that far time when fiery darts forsake
   Jove sitting wrapped in clouds and darkling mist,
when rivers, used to run all-out with brimming banks
   to reach the ocean, stay their headlong foot,
when at long last the western sea calls off its waves
   from pounding Sicily's beach with seething surf,
then, too, that brass suspended in the neighbor tower
   will cease producing rude bombastic blasts.

XVI

When winds no longer whistle, seas no longer roar,
   when clouds no longer thunder, split by fire,
when saffron hue and rose forsake the rainbow arch
   from head to toe of Thaumas' cloud-born child,
when shining fish the sea, when painted shells the shores,
   when shade the thick-grown groves deserts,
then, sweet Cornelius, from your belfry brassy bells
   will cease to belt their raucous noise.

COMMENTARY and NOTES

CL I

Genre: elegy (with pastoral allegory).
Meter: elegiac couplet.
Literary linkage: Callimachus, Propertius, Virgil, Marcantonio Flaminio.
Synopsis: The story opens with a dramatic gesture. Casa summons a poet's ghost from the dead to curb another poet: the offender has rebuked a goodly old shepherd for leaving rural duties to live in Rome. The hills can do without him, Casa says, and the city needs his ministry to heal its moral ills.

Comment

The problem of Horace underlies the first poem, which Casa wrote in a genre—elegy—that Horace never used. One motive may be scholarly. Elegies under Horace's name had been reported as seen by his ancient biographer and dismissed as forgeries: *nam elegi volgares* (for the elegies were vulgar).[1] The notice might have piqued a scholarly poet into a literary game: he would imagine a proper elegy worthy of Horace; certainly it would not reflect the values of the *vulgus*, the crowd that he and Horace despised.

More specific motives emerge from the first words. When Casa opens by calling the "Shades of Flaminio" to come to his aid, his "Flaminii Manes" evokes "Callimachi Manes" at the start of Propertius's third book. That was the moment when the Roman elegist was moving beyond his previous focus on love in response to the books of *Odes* just produced by Horace, his older contemporary. Propertius called on

---

[1] Suetonius, *Vita Horati*, 67–70: "Venerunt in manus meas et elegi sub titulo eius et epistula prosa oratione quasi commendantis se Maecenati, ed utraque falsa puto; nam elegi volgares, epistula etiam obscura, quo vitio minime tenebatur" in Augusto Rostagni, *Suetonio de Poetis* (Turin, 1964), brought to my attention by Professor Matthew Santirocco.

Callimachus, the Alexandrian Greek elegist,[2] for permission to enter sacred groves and assume the authority of a prophet and priest in emulation of Horace's vatic gravity.[3] Where before Propertius had centered elegy on erotic themes and repeatedly resorted to topics of demurral (*recusatio*), holding back from more ambitious, less personal subjects, now he was seeking to rise to the Horatian ethical and didactic plane, if not yet the prophetic and public voice.[4] Thus he offered a highly relevant program to Casa, who also needed to put love behind for a higher plane and rapprochment with Horace. Casa, too, is looking for a new gravity and measure, seeking distance from his early erotic forays and his frustrated fling with curial ambition.

By calling up Flaminio, Casa evokes a poetic range that runs from personal letters and epigrams through pastoral elegies, solemn odes, and sacred hymns, even to the Psalms of David transformed into Horatian meters.[5] Flaminio's poetry, says Casa, has the power to check the *malum carmen* of Priuli, a phrase that may suggest not merely "wicked song" but even "evil spell."[6] Priuli's piece, as Casa reports it, combines themes and voices of satire and Virgilian pastoral for its message that the old shepherd must leave corrupting urban love and go back to his country wife and rural flock. Against this extreme advice, Casa with and

---

[2] Callimachus (fl. c.3 BCE) lived in Cyrene and Alexandria and was a founder of the classical tradition of book-poetry through his *Aitia* and *Iambi*, which influenced the formation of Roman elegy by Catullus, Cornelius Gallus, Propertius, and Ovid: see Mario Puelma, "Die Aitien des Kallimachos als Vorbild der römischen Amores-Elegie," *Museum Helveticum* 39 (1982): 1–46, 287–304.

[3] "Book III with its signs of movement upward to a middle ground in the stylistic hierarchy: first the elaborate adaptation of Hesiodic-Callimachean myths of poetics to erotic elegy, and the implicit challenge to Horace's Roman Odes, then more generally the allusions to the *Georgics* rather than the *Bucolics*, and the moralizing interest which appears to reflect the influence of Horace's *Satires* as well as *Odes*": John Van Sickle, "Propertius (*uates*): Augustan Ideology, Topography, and Poetics in *Eleg.* IV,1," *Dialoghi di Archeologia* 8 (1975): 119. "The self-indulgence of the subjective elegist immersed in his personal feelings, often a retrospective and escapist posture however ironically maintained, yields before the broader critical impulses of the poet commenting on his peers and on means of communication between people. We now contemplate the vivid abstractions that rule our lives, the relationship between style and ethics and, generally, social as much as sexual *mores*": M. C. J. Putnam, "Propertius' Third Book: Patterns of Cohesion," in John Van Sickle, ed., Augustan Poetry Books, issue of *Arethusa* 13 (1980): 98. The portrait could be that of Casa.

[4] Also in the third book, further emulating the *Odes*, Propertius made a carefully ordered sequence.

[5] *Marci Antonii Joannis Antonii et Gabrielis Flaminiorum Forocorneliensium Carmina* (Prati: Typis Raynerii Guasti, 1831), 2 vols., a reprinting of the edition by F. M. Mancurtius (Padua: Cominus, 1727).

[6] Carmina, "charms," are incantations meant to compel a lover to leave the city for the country in Virgil, *Bucolics* 8.

through Flaminio proposes a middle ground: not rural retreat pure and simple, but also not just unbridled ambition in town. Like Horace, Casa prefers a mean between extremes. In genre, Casa thus produces pastoral elegy, which echoes the middle of Flaminio's poetic range, somewhere between epigrams and hymns.

Notes
1–8: call the dead poet to witness the offense of the living poet.
1. **Flamin**: Marcantonio Flaminio (1498–1550), the prolific writer of sacred and secular poetry, confidant of reform-minded clergy. *Flaminii Manes*: cf. *Callimachi Manes* (Shades of Callimachus) in Propertius, *Eleg.* III.1.1.
2. **Elysian fields**: in Greco-Roman mythology, that part of the underworld where the blessed dwell, especially ancient heroes, kings, and bards, e.g., in Virgil, *Georgics* 1.38, *Aeneid* 6.545, 638–78. By contrast, when Flaminio imagined his own afterlife in the poem of farewell to his friend Priuli (see v. 5), he placed himself in the Christian heaven above (*Carm.* VI.36: discussed in the Introduction, part II). Casa's pagan mythology typifies the secular humanism that scandalized northern reformers like Erasmus but expressed the Italian pride in the Roman heritage that often served to compensate for real political setbacks.[7] The theme of Italian pride re-echoes in *CL* VI.68; IX.58; XII.2, 6, 8, 32, 40.
3. **Cocytus**: a river in the underworld (Greek: lamenting), not exclusive to Virgil, but used by him repeatedly in accounts of the world of death.
5. **Priuli**: Alvise Priuli (1470–1560), idealistic Venetian nobleman and cleric, long-time secretary of Reginald Cardinal Pole (1500–1558), a friend and patron of Flaminio. To Priuli Flaminio addressed a dying farewell (see note on v.2).
7. **Galat**: Galeazzo Florimonte (ca.1478–1567), bishop of Aquino (between Rome and Naples), summoned in 1550 by Pope Julius III to serve as his secretary, long an intimate of Priuli and Casa: see Introduction II.

9–28: question and refute the offender.
11–12. **hill town ... smoke-grimed country shrines**: the country con-

---

[7] Denys Hays, *Intellectual Tendencies: Literature: The Printed Book*, in G. R. Elton, ed., *New Cambridge Modern History* (Cambridge: Cambridge University Press, 1990), 2:374.

trasted with the city, in a pastoral allegory that implies a conflict between the demands of the Roman curia and the needs of the diocese in the hills.

15–16. **healing hands on rulers or the city**: the city and the papal court represent moral sickness in the moralizing version of pastoral that gained currency from Petrarch, who himself withdrew to his rural retreat.[8] Casa argues that pastoral virtue is needed in the city.

17–18. **highest guard of groves**: the pastoral trope expands to include the pope as supreme shepherd.

19. **Melfi**: the river at Aquino.

22. **Hyblaean honeycombs**: bees of Sicily and Attica were fabled: cf. Virgil, *Bucolics* 1.54.

23. **Amaryllis**: a pastoral sweetheart, most prominently in Virgil, *Bucolics* 1.5, but without the theme of moral correction. Virgil's Amaryllis was read by some ancient commentators allegorically as a symbol of Rome (so Servius). For Casa, she represents the Roman curia.

29–34: flatter the dead poet and call him to help silence the offender.

29–34. **come here** (*huc ades*): a pathetic prayer in Virgil, *Bucolics* 2.45. The theme of Flaminio's merit closes, as it opened, the elegy.

CL II

Genre: satire.
Meter: dactylic hexameter.
Literary linkage: Horace (Euripides).
Synopsis: The prayer for healing turns out to have a personal motive. Casa confesses to the old shepherd that he himself suffers from the city's moral disease. Like Helen in Greek tragedy, he cannot get free of whorish pride. He lays the blame on the urban crowd: their flattery infected him with ambition. He feels like one that is trying to return from long exile. Diagnosis provokes despair. Unable to get rid of the plague and save himself, he calls stern friends to act and carry out a radical cure: drive him from Rome. Only by leaving the place of infection can he get away from the disease.

---

[8] David R. Coffin, *The Villa in the Life of Renaissance Rome* (Princeton: Princeton University Press, 1979), 9–10.

Comment

In calibrating his poetics so carefully, Casa presupposes the classical tradition of defining and ranking genres and modes each type with its own specific meter, theme, tone, and ranking. Organized vertically, by analogy with social classes, the system placed at the top genres like hymns and heroic epic, which used "high" style for divinities and upper class figures. Relegated to the lower end of the spectrum and "low" style was a somewhat heterogeneous cluster that included not only personal lyric and pastoral and erotic elegy with their focus on love, but also moral and literary satire, comedy, and any form devoted to ordinary folk and personal voices. On such a traditional scale, Casa moves downward in his second poem, into vivid personal confession that turns into conversation with friends: in short, satire as practiced by Horace. For his elaborate and forceful opening simile he draws on tragedy, comparing his depravity to Helen's, whom Euripides represented in the *Orestes* as so infected with pride in her looks that she hesitated to sacrifice a lock of hair on her sister's tomb lest the loss make her look less seductive to lechers.

Notes

1–24: ambition as a lingering disease.

1. **As Helen**: the scathing image of Helen as slow to give up her sexual allure echoes Euripides' *Orestes*, vv. 94–129, where Electra bitterly comments on Helen. Casa adapts and elaborates the polemic for satirical emphasis: his theme and style descend from the heroic echo of Troy, through the unheroic husband, the halting sacrifice, to the stinging last low word, *moechis* (adulterers, rakes) in a rhetorical spectacular.
   when Troy was taken: less emphatically focused than the opening of *CL* I, this phrase yet signals a shift in genre and poetic authority from Propertian elegy to Horace, who used a similar formula twice in hexameters: "capta ... Troia" (*Satires* II.3.191) and "captae post tempora Troiae" (*Ars Poetica* 141).
3. **Clytemnestra**: Helen's dead sister was owed a ritual sacrifice of hair. She killed her husband, Agamemnon, on his return from capturing Troy provoking her son Orestes to kill her and avenge his father.
9. **Galat**: old shepherd and moral healer (cf. I.7).
14–15. **lust or ... ambition**: rhetorical opposition masks psychological identity, for Casa has an erotic history of his own. Ambition left him *saucius* (pricked, wounded), which is a common meta-

phor for erotic torment, e.g., Virgil, *Aeneid* 4.1. Casa's flamboyant comparison with Helen displays the same intensely dramatic sensibility with which he transformed the Petrarchan tradition in Italian lyric (Saccone, *Le buone e le cattive maniere*, 117). Casa saw his life as discontinuous, broken by moral exile (*Rime* 47.10–17: "Pitiful tale to tell what I suffered in such long exile wandering abroad"), unlike Bembo's continuous development through life to ever fuller satisfactions (Ley, "Die 'scienza civile'" 216–17).

16. **shame**: *pudor* here has the sense of shame or modesty. Yet Casa also feels *pravus pudor* (corrupt shame), which is fear of the opinion of the crowd (see *CL* II.22–24).

25–50: anatomy of ambition—praised by the crowd, it lacks substance. Show does not value make.

35. **Gout**: suffered by Casa severely in his hands.

42. **Faerno**: Gabriele Faerno (d. 1562), scholar-poet and functionary of the Vatican Library. On his poetry and scholarship, see Anthony Grafton, *Joseph Scaliger: A Study in the History of Classical Scholarship* (Oxford, 1983), 65ff.

43. **formed ill and ill alert**: "informis ... inque | excussus," a pairing reinforced by the repeated negating prefix; the second *in-* stands at the verse end, separated from the world it negates; the sense thus emphasized, "not shaped or composed (as a work of literary art)" (which is the meaning of the Latin verb *excudere*, *excussus* here), complements the aesthethic and ethical implications of *informis*, "not endowed with lovely form."

46. **burning shakes**: continues the trope of ambition as disease.

51–60: a call to friends for cure by expulsion from the city.

51. **trim at the root the golden curl**: recalls and applies the opening simile in a self-dramatizing gesture, begging friends to remedy sickness by expulsion, that brings to mind Oedipus cursing himself and pleading for exile. Casa tempers para-tragic emphasis by the homely parable of the mule in the manner of Horatian satire.

53–54. **Priuli, Pole**: the intimate circle to which Flaminio belonged (see *CL* I.1, 5 and Introduction, part II).

CL III

Genre: epistle.
Meter: dactylic hexameter.
Literary linkage: Horace.
Synopsis: Shifting to a mood of self-defense, Casa defines an alternative to ambition. By way of an example, he eulogizes a friend: Bembo's life, he says, is ruled by wisdom, although the crowd demeans it as a form of "idleness, lack of care." Such "idleness" does have its literary and erotic sins, Casa admits; but he insists that these are harmless, private, and forgiveable, when compared to the ambitious public vices of his critics. They constitute the city's true infection and danger. He closes with renewed praise for the simple poetic life as superior to ambition.

Comment

Continuing in hexameter, Casa modulates to a blend of florid encomium and self-defense. The altered theme and tone suggest the alternative mode of Horace's own hexameters: no longer the rougher satires but the more genteel and theoretical epistles. It is their discursive manner and philosophical position that Casa recaptures in his praise of Bembo for *sophia* (wisdom) and in his defense of *desidia* (idleness, lack of care). In closing he renews his praise for the simple virtue of the poetic life and cites the example of a poet like Bandinelli. He has found in his own previous life and art something like the erotic concerns of Propertius's earlier elegies and pastoral's traditional leisure for poetry and love; likewise he invokes the traditional defense of elegy and pastoral: that they are free of the hurtful greed and ambition that corrupt the city.

Notes

1–21: praise for the exemplary life of Bembo, rich in wisdom and talent, shared by Casa, against vulgar opinion and the carping crowd.

1–2. **wisdom ... ability**: an ethical and poetic ideal.

6. **stupid crowd**: heavy reemphasis on contempt for the *ignarum vulgus*, a motif that will recur and become basic to the moral and aesthetic position that Casa works out; also one of his basic debts to Horace (e.g., *Carm*. III.1.1: "I hate the profane crowd").

10. **no sane man**: health equated with discriminating between vulgar and elite opinion. One symptom of moral illness in Casa's self-diagnosis was his susceptibility to the crowd (cf. II.21–24).

12. **Bembo**: after a full picture of the values and attitudes admired,

14-15. **we get charged with sloth by folks:** Casa identifies himself with Bembo; their shared ideal comes under attack as "sloth" (*desidia*) by the ambitious crowd. One energetic attack on Casa came in 1546 from Pietro Paolo Vergerio (1498-1565), whom Casa persecuted for reformist heresy.

17. **trifling verse:** *versiculi* was a diminutive used in self-deprecating poetics by Horace and Catullus (cf. *CL* X.1 with note); *nugae* occurred with similar effect in Catullus, *Carm.* 1.4.

22-44: *blame the crowd for three types of vicious life—shyster lawyer, inheritance chaser, corrupt governor.*

45-82: *even admitting to faults on both sides, Casa's style of life harms no one.*

45. **You blaze, ambitious, fired:** metaphors of fire, traditional for sexual passion, here get applied to ambition. The parallelism of the passions was implicit already in *CL* II.14.

46. **purple:** rich dyes were a traditional mark of luxury and conspicuous consumption; in the ecclesiastical world, the purple symbolizes the cardinalate, which was an object of ambition and major cause of frustration for Casa.

66. *veternus:* the word ends with rather than within the line's third foot, a rhythm rare in hexameter poetry and unique in Casa. The lack of the expected pause causes the reader to stumble and then reflect on how the rough rhythm suits the theme of "heavy torpor, old age."

69-70. **wealth my careful father:** piety towards the parent, a major motif in Horace's self-image, appears only here. Casa's relations with his father were strained.

76. *trabe,:* omitting the comma here or adding further commas at the verse end would point up the logical relations of the clauses.

77-78. *quam ... intereo;:* how much more helpful to a modern reader if punctuated by an exclamation point!

78-79. **Apollo's Muses or fine love:** the central combination in Casa's ideal, as also exemplified by Bembo.

81. *viro:* "with venom," translated as ablative singular following Lucretius 2.853: *suo contractans perdere uiro* (tainting by its own tang to spoil).

83-101: *Casa does not bark vainly, and he gives praise where due.*

83. *egerit: Itur*: here direct speech begins, signaled only by the colon and capital letter in the copy text.
85-86. **Quirin's hill or Aventine**: Casa thinks of the two hills facing each other across the valley of the Circus Maximus, the Palatine, associated with Romulus-Quirinus, and the Aventine, associated with Romulus's twin, Remus. In the northwest sector of the Palatine, Casa's patron, Cardinal Farnese, created a sumptuous garden in the relics of the Roman emperors' palace.
88. **Bargul**: mentioned by Livy (29.12.13) and a place in Illyria of no account.
95. **Molsa**: Francesco Maria Molza (1489-1544; see Introduction, part II): poet, rake, protegé of Cardinal Farnese. His poetry appears with that of Casa, Faerno, and Flaminio in the manuscript anthology from Florence now in Munich (described as *1560*, Introduction, part IV), and with Casa, Faerno, and Priuli in Ubaldino's anthology (1563, Introduction, part IV), which includes his fierce elegy in the person of Catherine of Aragon against Henry VIII, who was the nemesis of his friend Pole (cf. *CL* II).
96. **Pieria**: region in Thessaly sacred to the Muses.
96. **Camena**: Italian water goddess, identified as an Italic equivalent for the Muses by Roman poets from the beginning of their literature. Casa takes learned pains to attribute Latin as well as Greek authority to his friend and to emphasize Italian values.
97. **Ubaldin**: Ubaldino Bandinelli (d. 1551) left his library to Casa. He found Bembo pompously mannered and said so, provoking Bembo to incite Aretino to satirize him (see Lorenzo Campana, "Monsignor Giovanni della Casa e i suoi tempi," *Studi storici* [Pisa], XVI [1907]: 24).
91-101. The closing display of Horatian equanimity papers over contradictions that must have been acute when Casa composed the epistle in 1535 (see Introduction, part II). Molza was a rascal. Ubaldino disprized Bembo. In any event, all three were dead by the time of Casa's crisis and retreat: Molza since 1544, Bembo since 1547, and Ubaldino in 1551. The theme of harmful and harmless passions survives to find its place in the emergent context of the book. For the linkage in humanist ideology between poetic and ethical values, see Anthony Grafton and Lisa Jardine, *From Humanism to the Humanities* (Cambridge, Mass.: Harvard University Press, 1986), passim.

CL IV

Genre: iambic (epode).
Meter: pure iambic trimeter [3 ia//].
Literary linkage: Euripides (Archilochus), Horace.
Synopsis: On the offensive again, Casa redoubles his polemical force and directs it specifically now against women. He reviles woman's very name and nature, which he treats as a prime cause of the social ills he denounced in the city and himself. His onslaught is so violent as to divert attention to his own nature and suggest that he has a penchant for dramatic poses and blaming others, whether the flattering crowd or hypocritical critics. The more tempted and seduced he feels, the more he blames and derides. By this standard, the threat of careerist ambition is relatively slight: it seduced him only in mid-life. Women fascinated him earlier and longer.

Comment

Declamatory rather than conversational, the polemic carries Casa to a new pitch. He has chosen a short passage that builds two charges against women: lustfulness and wastefulness. Twice already he has used lust figuratively: he identified Helen's insatiability with his own ambition (in *CL* II); and he contrasted the woman of the city, Amaryllis (sc. the Roman curia), who required tutelage and stern examples, with the woman in the country (sc. diocese in the hills), who had been taught chastity and could afford to give up her shepherd/husband (sc. bishop, in *CL* I).

This new polemical force comes with a shift in genre, from satire to one of its progenitors and cohorts. The vituperative thrust and iambic meter mark the attack as an epode of the most virulent strain, with ties to comedy, imprecation, and curse, which lured the young Horace into two experiments, likewise attacking women—early pieces against a lecherous crone and a witch (*Epodes* 8 and 17, the latter composed in the iambs Casa used here). Casa also has the precedent of Francesco Berni, as well as the frequent attacks on women in writers like Boccaccio, and his own tract against marrying, which emphasized the luxuriousness of women (Santosuosso *Vita*, 48–60). Also, as he had in *CL* II, Casa draws on tragedy for dramatic punch, here translating from Euripides' *Hippolytus* the hero's infamous diatribe against the female kind. The tragic models serve as vehicles for Casa's strongest and most conflicted feelings.

Notes

1–9: children are better bought than produced by women.

1. **why must they say ...** : translated from Euripides, *Hippolytus* (616–50, omitting 651–68). Casa renders thirty-five Greek verses into thirty-eight in Latin, following rather closely. In the drama, the celibate hero has just learned from a servant that his stepmother lusts for him; his reaction begins with this diatribe. Casa adopts it without frame, identifying the hero's voice with his own persona. He put greater distance between himself and the tragic character in the Helen simile (*CL* II.1–8), framing the satirical moment from Euripides as a figure of speech in an imagined talk with a friend. Casa had written a youthful tract in praise of celibacy.

10–22: women waste wealth of fathers and husbands.

23–31: best the woman of least quality, worst the clever, with her erotic scheming.

30. **Cypris**: the goddess from Cyprus, Greek Aphrodite, Latin Venus, equated with sexual love; cf. *Veneris ... cupidine* (lust to make love, *CL* II.14), and *rem ... in Venerem effundam* (spill wealth for lust, III.69); in short, Casa perceives instability and danger in female sexuality.

32–38: women corrupt servants and spread gossip.

CL V

Genre: epode.
Meter: dactylic hexameter + iambic dimeter [6 da.// + 2 ia//].
Literary linkage: Horace, *Epodes* 2.
Synopsis: Blaming builds towards action and moves the story along. On the crest of his polemics, Casa declares that he will leave Rome. He takes responsibility, no longer calling on others to drive him out. To his moral reasons for going, he adds a physical argument, describing himself as old and stricken by gout, eager to exchange a pestilential Roman climate for a more salubrious Venice. Yet fascination with Rome threatens to break his resolve. The very act of saying farewell makes him reflect on what he will miss: Rome's cultural brilliance and historic grandeur, above all its legendary water, flowing fresh and cool, which provokes the discouraging thought of a fetid draft

from a Venetian cistern. He renews resolve by claiming the high ground of civic order: in Venice, he says, the constitutional climate is balanced and proper, war is subject to civilian control, and Prudence both obeys and rules. He caps this argument to himself with a political myth from Greece and Rome: Justice leaving human society as the Iron Age began and returning for a renewed Golden Age. In his version of the myth, Justice flees corrupt Italy and takes refuge in the ideal republic of Venice.

Comment

For his declaration of resolve to seek a remedy in Venice, Casa turns to a less venomous kind of epode. On the scale of style and theme, he moves to a seriousness of tone and to social and political themes that compare with Horace's more ambitious and prophetic pieces (*Epodes* 1, 7, 9, 14, 16). Casa's story of retreat, however, most closely parallels Horace's second epode with its parable of the money-lender who called in loans and left the greedy city for the simpler pleasures of country life, which Horace elaborates in full detail only to undercut abruptly at the end, saying that his man was back in town by the end of the month and the money out again in loans. In Casa's case reversal was not to be so comical and quick.

Notes

1–8: resolve to leave for Venice, more salubrious than the territory around Rome, better for a body aging and afflicted by gout.

1–2. **Tyrrheni ... Lati**: from the Tyrrhenian Sea off central Italy, the wind brings rain to the region around Rome, *Latium* (Italian *Lazio*), which is no longer so disease ridden, since the coastal marshes have been cleared. With artful emphasis, Casa defines his posture, placing key terms of place in important positions: "Tyrrheni" before the caesura in the hexameter, "Lati" at verse end in the dimeter, then the Venetians directly after himself, "me," revealed as the one in flight. Geographically and politically, Latium for Casa implies Farnese power, both the papacy of Paul III and the Farnese possessions just north of Rome. The decline of their fortunes has made the territory politically less favorable to Casa: he expresses his disillusionment in terms of climate, health, and age.

3–6. **breezes**: *auræ salubriores*, not winds, and more healthful for the aging and unhealthy poet.

age and ... gout: although only forty-eight years old in 1551,

Casa had long suffered gout in his hands. He vacillated about going (letter to Ludovico Beccadelli, who succeeded him as nuncio in Venice, 15 April 1551, *Opere* [1806] 4:379); by September he was in Venice.

8. **Faerno**: the scholarly and poetic friend typifies the society that Casa leaves with regret (cf. *CL* II.43, and vv. 11–12 below).

9–26: remembers Rome's merits, brilliant people and monuments of glory, wines and water, by contrast with the very inferior water supply at Venice.

27–41: but, Venice excels in hospitality, respect for law and order, peace: ideal commonwealth, where justice, driven out of Italy, finds refuge.

37. **Justice ... found a home**: *æquum*; Justice left when human society declined into the Iron Age, only to return with the Golden Age, according certain mythic traditions: cf. Virgil, *Bucolics* 4.6. Casa compresses the myth and uses it to draw a flattering contrast between the rest of Italy (where his Farnese patrons are momentarily in retreat) and the Republic of Venice. Resurgent Farnese influence will let him project the myth onto Italy once again (*CL* IX, then XI, XII, XIII). For other appropriations of the myth, see Frances Yates, *Astraea* (London, 1975, 1985).

39. **West**: *Hesperia* (western land), brought into play by Virgil in the *Aeneid*, calling it the old Greek name for Italy. As a generic term, it served Virgil to suggest the promised land, which gradually through prophecy was revealed to the exiled hero Aeneas. It acquired associations also with the mythic Golden Age. The Virgilian idea of a "promised land" underlies Casa's choice of the term just when he feels that promise and hope are lost (cf. the tones altered by changing political circumstances in *CL* IX.29 and then *CL* XII.1).

CL VI

Genre: lyric (ode).
Meter: Asclepiad [type 2].
Literary linkage: Horace.
Synopsis: The move from Rome to Venice marks a turning point in the story. Far at last from corrupting influence, secure in an environment he could idolize as ethically supportive, Casa begins by reaffirming the ideal of literary life and the value of writing. His first

poem from exile commemorates a Florentine humanist who exemplified the cultural alternative to ambition: both poet and teacher, Ubaldino Bandinelli figured along with Bembo as an example of the literary ideal that Casa defended for himself in the third poem. Now he gives the ideal new emphasis in the oxymoronic expressions *operosa otia* (busy leisure) and *quies gnaua* (industrious ease), which suggest a program both ethical and aesthetic for Casa's reformed life.

Comment

Signaling his break with corruption and arrival in the morally curative place, Casa moves up and across the grid of Horatian poetics to produce the solemn and dignified ode commemorating Bandinelli, marking his upward progress by echoing the ode that Horace directed to Virgil on the death of a literary friend (*Carm.* I.24.1-4). Horace's choice of meter determined Casa's: the second type within the group of lyric meters known as Asclepiadean.[1]

Notes

1-8: praise owed now; longing has not grown less, although too much time has passed since the death.

1. **To one so dear**: the pointed allusion to Horace addressing Virgil on measure in grief:
   Quis desiderio sit pudor aut modus
   tam cari capitis? praecipe lugubris
   cantus, Melpomene, cui liquidam pater
      vocem cum cithara dedit.
            Carm. I.24.1-4
   (What shame or measure ought to check desire
   for one so dear? Supply the mournful chants,
   Melpomene: to you your father gave
      clear voice and lyre.)
   As in *CL* I and II, the echo of a famous classical poem signals a progression in genre, here inaugurating the cycle of odes. From the same ode, Priuli adapted one phrase for a very different theme: where Horace told Virgil that he could not persuade death, even if he played the lyre "more coaxingly than Thracian Orpheus," Priuli remonstrated with a girl for rejecting a poet, even though he "measured songs with an Etruscan lyre more coaxingly than Thracian Orpheus" (in Johannes Paulus Ubal-

---

[1] D. R. Shackleton Bailey, *Horatius Opera* (Stuttgart: Teubner, 1985), 333-34.

dinus, ed., *Carmina poetarum nobilium studio conquisita* [Milan: Antonius Antonianus, 1563], 24v).

3. **threnody**: *Næniam*, the old Latin song of grief, here a specific sign of the plaintive mode within the lyric genre.

9–16: Ubaldino rich in morality, wisdom, literary achievements, not in gold or purple that create greedy anxiousness.

9–12. The values are those praised in Bembo, Molza, and Ubaldino himself (*CL* III.1–12, 95–97). Casa revels in the paradoxical juxtaposition of opposites, *quies gnava* (calm intensity) and *operosa otia* (repose ... employed), the busy, productive leisure of the arts: leisure because not engaged with worldly ambitions, hence the ultimate paradox, underlined by the concluding word *diuitem* (wealthy), but not because of worldly goods, as also in the earlier praise of Ubaldino (*CL* III.100). Leisure is a defining topic of the pastoral trope, e.g., Virgil, *Bucolics* 1.6: "A god made this leisure *haec otia* for us."

17–28: greed and vanity exemplified: the origin of gold traced to divine tormentor, Mercury.

24–25. **god of commerce Mercury**: Casa actually writes "god descended from Atlas," which the translation decodes and relates to the thematic texture.

29–36: gold not needed by the truly good, who stand on their own, firm (like Ubaldino), while fortune makes abrupt shifts.

30–31. **Greece ... Aegean**: generic names where Casa mentioned a specific mountain and island, Pelion and Carpathos.

33. **firm ... frail**: alliteration easy enough since Casa used Latin words that migrated into English.

37–44: Ubaldino well supplied in riches of Latin and Greek, hence mourned all the more because such stores lost to death.

37–38. **Latium ... Greeks**: the two classical cultures. "Latium" here implies the Latin-Roman literary heritage, which in Casa's sympathies complements the geographical and political implications to which he gives primary emphasis in other contexts: *CL* V.2; VIII.22; XII.12, 44 (with notes).

41. **Arno ... Arno**: doubling the name, Casa intensifies the expressive effect. He identifies Florence by its etymology—"in flower."

43. **treasure-troves of mind**: learning likened to "heaped up wealth" in a metaphor from the business world of Casa's father who guaranteed the son's ease: cf. *CL* III.69–70, "wealth my careful father made." The always practical Florentines were am-

bivalent towards the tradition of rural retreat: the country should produce food and culture should glorify the city (Coffin, *Villa*, 10–11).

45–56: the cultural loss compared to the destruction of a richly laden merchant ship, which was greedy and unlucky in the end.

45–56. A simile in Horace's grandest manner. The catalogue of luxuries lost threatens to overwhelm the focus on modesty. By the end, it seems that scholarship, too, has suffered a reversal. The ethical life proves to be as vulnerable as the life of greed to Fortune's shifts.

57–68: may the name of Ubaldino survive in this poetry since he taught me the art.

57. **golden child of Jove**: the Muse, Melpomene, addressed also at the start. The use of ring composition marks Casa's style:

   CL I, the opening call to the dead poet and closing prayer that he act;

   CL II, the opening image of Helen's reluctance to cut her curl and closing appeal that friends cut Casa's curl;

   CL III, the initial praise of Bembo and final praise of Molsa and Ubaldino.

   CL V, the initial praise of physical healthfulness and final praise of civic health.

   Further, more specialized, study of Casa's ring structures and how they relate to those of Horace would need to incorporate the subtle and illuminating considerations by R. J. Tarrant, "*Da Capo* Structures in Some Odes of Horace," in *Homage to Horace: A Bimillenary Celebration*, ed. S. J. Harrison (Oxford: Clarendon Press, 1995), 3–49.

61. **Castalian path**: named for the spring on Mt. Parnassus above Delphi, sacred to Apollo. Frequently signals Casa's pride in the Greek origins of his poetry."Reading the poets" primed the pump for the odes (Letter to Pier Vettori: 2 March 1552, *Opere* [1806] 4:158).

61–62. **he taught ... he taught**: *docuit*, one verb, does duty for two clauses introducing a key theme in the narratives by which poets define their origins and aims, e.g., Horace corrected by Quirinus (*Serm.* I.10.31–35); Virgil encouraged by Caesar Octavian (*Bucolics* 1.6, 44–45), then reduced by Apollo (*Bucolics* 6.3–51); Propertius taught by Love (*Eleg.* I.1.5); and the similar themes in Theocritus, Callimachus, and Hesiod. By thus praising Ubaldino, Casa furnishes his own venture into lyric with an authoritative origin.

68. **Italian pride**: the *decus Italiae* (ornament in which Italy takes pride) is Ubaldino, redounding to the glory of Florence and of Casa's lyric muse. Similarly honorific, Virgil addressed the nascent world hero as *decus hoc aeui* (this pride of the age) in *Bucolics* 4.11, which re-echoed in honorific contexts of the *Aeneid*, among them *decus Italiae uirgo* to Camilla (maiden pride of Italy, 11.508).

Casa makes the ode a vehicle to recast and defend once more his ethical and aesthetic values (cf. *CL* III), shifting from autobiography and self-criticism (*CL* II–V) and putting his Roman dilemmas behind as he ventures into the more grave, more abstract, more confident mode of lyric, for which he provides an authoritative origin. Yet the rejected world intrudes: the most overwhelming part of the poem is the comparison between Ubaldino's death and a greedy trader lost, much as the image of Helen's reluctance overshadowed other arguments (*CL* II), or as a pastoral retreat comes to an unruly climax in images of rape (Horace, *Carm.* I.17.22–28).

CL VII

Genre: lyric (ode).
Meter: Asclepiad [type 3].
Literary linkage: Horace.
Synopsis: Following the example of Bandinelli, Casa takes up the role of mentor. He sets out to warn his nephew against flattery, which he likens vividly to insidious stepmothers, to a seductive girl, with "swelling nipples and soft lap," and to bait that lures a songbird into a hidden trap.

Comment

The most widely and variously circulated of the odes (see Introduction, parts II and IV).

For his warning against flattery's seductive power Casa chose another Asclepiadean meter—the third. Horace had paired it with the second type three times in his first book of odes, each a poem that conveys a plea: warning against moral shipwreck, in love and allegorically in life (*Carm.* I.5 and 14), and warning against unnatural shyness towards timely openness to love (*Carm.* I.23). When Casa compares flattery to a temptress, the new moralist evokes the temptations of the old roué.

He uses particularly expressive language—*turgidulas papillas* (swelling little nipples) and *molli sinu* (soft bend of bosom)—recalling the highly sensuous poems in which Catullus described his mistress's sparrow, hopping about in her lap, and her eyes swollen from weeping at the bird's death (*Carm* 2.3).

Notes

1–4: like wicked stepmothers' honeyed venom, flattery destroys the trusting mind.

2. **no otherwise than stepmothers**: their poisoning ways were proverbial: cf. Ovid, *Metamorphoses* 1.147; Horace, *Epod.* 5.9; and Juvenal 6.403. To a friend, Casa wrote, "As for the comparison of the stepmother, I wanted to say 'Flattery knows how to destroy the mind no differently than stepmothers when they sweeten with honey death-dealing dishes', which comparison would be whole and complete if I had said further: 'know how to destroy stepsons'." In this form, the comparison won praise, he adds, and, "however distant, it does not seem far-fetched, since just as the sweetness of the words covers the harm done by the adjectives, so the honey of the dishes covers the poison the stepmothers put in": Casa (Venice) to Astore Paleotto (Florence), 1 March 1552 (Santosuosso, "Inediti casiani," 493–94). Omitting the fourth term of comparison pleased his friends, Casa adds, since the next verse repeats and explains the comparison, assigning to the murmurs of flattery the same effects as stepmothers give their poisons: "And I believe that the poets, especially of lyric, take regard to leave a little desire in the mind of the readers, which sometimes adds novelty and dignity to writings." Here he cites a similar case where Horace clearly considered an incomplete comparison more satisfying than a complete one ("nel primo libro Carmina 16 che comincia: O matre pulchra").

5–16: desire truth and praise that has been earned.

5. **venom**: cf. *CL* III.81 with note.

17–32: as sex attracts, so does praise, yet worth must not depend on it.

17. **Compare a young man's inward feelings**: betrays and expects erotic experience, in language that suggests intimacy with Catullus.

18. *candida*: cf. Catullus's epithet for a gleaming mistress, *Carm.* 13.4; 35.8; 68.70.

turgidulas: cf. Catullus's precious diminutive for his mistress's eyes swollen with weeping, *Carm.* 3.18.

19. **nulla veste papillas**: "with no garment nipples," cf. *reiecta veste papillas* (her garment thrown back, nipples) in Catullus, *Carm.* 66.81.
21. **so praises coax the mind**: the fourth term of the comparison spelled out (despite the aesthetic principles cited above, on v. 1), then even explained and amplified by *uera ubi concinunt* (when even truths they magnify).

33-40: Deceitful praise is the trap.

38. **trifles**: *nugae*, also at v. 11, refers to trivial and empty speech, but at *CL* III.17 Casa uses it with self-deprecating irony for his "verselets" and other literary missives, echoing Catullus's irony towards his book (*Carm.* 1.4).
38-40. An image of entrapment closes, as one opened: for previous ring structures, see *CL* VI.57 with note.

CL VIII

Genre: lyric (ode).
Meter: Asclepiad [type 1: Horace, *Carm.* I.1, III.30, IV.7].
Literary linkage: Horace (cf. "Fortune" in *Carm.* I.34, 35).
Synopsis: The ideal of a simple and unchanging life leads to preoccupation with the threat of change. Casa imagines his composure shaken by the swings of Fortune, which he portrays as a fickle power that arbitrarily upsets both good and bad conditions. He wants none of that, preferring steady simplicity. Change could only be for the worse. Let Fortune keep clear of his humble dwelling.

Comment

For the theme of Fortune's changes, too, Horace offered a precedent (*Carm.* I. 34, 35, both in Alcaic meter). Casa made a distinctive innovation. He chose to continue in the Asclepiadean series but shift to a type that Horace reserved for rare and distinctive roles. He used this so-called first type only three times in the four books of odes: to open and close the entire structure of the first three books, then at the center of the fourth book. In theme Casa's rejection of Fortune parallels Horace's opening poem, which catalogues the futile ambitions of others and declares Horace's own contentment with his poetic calling, which he describes as a rural retreat that may bring him fame as a bard. Another parallel is only implicit. Horace dedicates his ode to his powerful patron Maecenas. When Casa's patron, Alessandro Cardinal Farnese, requested an ode on the variability of Fortune, Casa initially demurred: see the letter of Casa (Venice) to Astorre Paleotti (Florence, in the house of Cardinal Farnese) in Appendix II, 1552.iii.1 (see also Introduction, part II).

Notes

1–3: Fortune lacks plan or purpose, merely changes.

1. **Devoid of purpose, Fortune:** the goddess does not appear by name in this poem (but is named at *CL* VI.34). The list of attributes reveals her identity. The opening phrase rings with Horatian gravity and paradox.

4–9: common praises of Fortune when she is good: beneficiaries credit her with the values of philosophy.

6–7. **child of goodly Jove:** like the address to Melpomene (*CL* VI.57), using the same word, *progenies*, which carries a solemn and archaic tone: cf. *maximi magna progenies Iouis* (great offspring of greatest Jove) in Catullus, *Carm.* 34.5–6, and *iam noua progenies* (now new child), in Virgil, *Bucolics* 4.7.

7–9. **reason ... wisdom ... worth:** the crowd assign the highest ethical values with the least real justification: once again the vulgar are Casa's whipping boy.

10–19: common complaints against Fortune when she is bad.

19–26: even when good, cannot be trusted, so let Fortune keep away from the poet's humble abode.

20–21. **little door:** *ostiolum*—the diminutive emphasizes the simplicity which is part of the conventional image of the literary life (cf. *CL* III.16; VI.9–13).

23. **Latium:** a nuance for Cardinal Farnese, who at this time was in Florence prudently withdrawn from Rome and his family's territories in upper Lazio: cf. the negative image of Latium at *CL* V.2, when Casa, too, felt the need to depart, and the more positive, specific Farnese associations later (*CL* XII.12, 44).

CL IX

Genre: lyric (ode).
Meter: Asclepiad (type 2: see Introduction, part III).
Literary linkage: Horace.
Synopsis: Casa's preoccupation with change was well founded: it now sweeps him quite away beyond the safe boundaries of his retreat. He

challenges his Muse to travel with him across the Alps. Together they will praise a Frenchman who has made Italy safe from contentious rulers by composing peace. The modest horizons of the poetic retreat expand. Reaching up and out, Casa assumes the role of public orator and prophet, announcing the reform of history. He stretches the myth of the Golden Age from Venice to encompass Italy, which he imagines now no longer fallen and corrupting, as when he left it for exile, but reformed and promising. One of his motives for retreat has been removed. Yet he makes a show of withdrawal and moderation to close, telling the Muse to pull back.

Comment

In three odes, Casa has used three different types from one metrical group, pairing two types that Horace paired, then turning to the type more rare and structurally significant for his most broad and politically delicate theme. In the present ode, Casa returns to the type with which he began—the second Asclepiad. His choice has structural point. By continuing with Asclepiads yet returning to the initial type, he defines a cycle and brings it to a close in a manner rivaling Horatian arrangement and unequalled by poets like Flaminio. In poetics, too, the ode marks a return and an advance. The opening metaphor of poetic travel across the Alps redefines the lyric mission announced as the cycle opened: Casa rises to vibrant praise of diplomatic success and a vision of the Golden Age restored to all Italy.

Notes

1-20: to his muse, a special mission, prayer that she show the way, assurance that this is no purchased praise.

1. **Where am I lofted**: the theme of upward movement suggests a rise in level after the satirical thrust of the Fortune ode.
   tollor: *vester in arduos | tollor Sabinos* (yours I am lofted to the steep Sabines) said Horace to his Latin Muses, the Camenae, in a complex evocation of his literary calling (*Carm.* III.4.21-22). Echoing Horace to outdo him, Casa announces a more ambitious goal, not the Sabine Hills near Rome but the distant, formidable Alps.

2. **Castalia's springs to cleanse**: the springs on Parnassus also figured in Casa's initial definition of lyric poetics at *CL* VI.61. Here he emphasizes the purity of the muse, in keeping with his own sense of poetry as a refuge from worldly pollution.

3-4. **kin | of mighty Jove**: *genus | magni Melpomene Iouis*, varies the address to the Muse, called "golden child of Jove who takes | delight in thunder" (*progenies aurea fulmine | gaudentis Iouis*) at *CL* VI.57–8; cf. the flattery of Fortune as "child of goodly | Jove" (*boni progenies Iouis*) at *CL* VIII.6.

5. **purple boots**: in honor of the cardinal's rank, cf. *CL* VIII.46.
7. *Soli: unus*: hiatus, at major pause in sense.
8. *pudor*: the sense of shame that exercised Casa especially in *CL* II.
9. **Your bard remind, o Goddess, of the way**: *Vatem diua tuum tu moneas uiæ*, a close appropriation of Virgil's solemn invocation for the second half of his epic: *tu uatem, tu, diua, mone* (you goddess, you remind the bard, *Aeneid* 7.41) Only here does Casa appropriate for himself the term *uates* that Virgil and Horace adapted to express their most ambitious poetic mission as public poets: by implication a pinnacle and turning point in the book.
10. *pure ... puer*: "boyhood ... pure," recalling Horace's own claim of initiation as a boy (*me ... puerum, Carm.* III.4.9–12), only that Casa weaves in a punning association between childhood and his moral concern.

21–32: comparison: a Spartan shepherd driving off a wolf compared to the cardinal going home with fame for defense of Italy.

27. **Tournon**: François Cardinal de Tournon (1489-1562)—nobleman, royal counselor and diplomat, militant and unbending prince of the church, defender and friend of Italy, collector of Greek manuscripts. Confidant of Francis I, he lost influence under Henry II, king from 1547 (see notes on *CL* XI and XII).
29. **the West**: again *Hesperia* with the aura of Virgilian myth, but now seen hopefully, restored to its role as a mythic promised land thanks to the diplomacy of De Tournon: politically, he made Italy more agreeable to Farnese interests, in which Casa placed renewed hopes: cf. *CL* V.39 and *CL* XII.1; also Introduction, part II.
29–32. For the variant version of this strophe, see Introduction, part IV.

33–40: he warned the fighters against Fortune's whirls and whims.

34. **Fortune**: presented as whirling, unstable again, also like a deceptive and seductive female; cf. *CL* VIII.
39. **embroidered**: the Latin *illusas* recalls a rare usage in Virgil, *Georgics* 2.464, *illusas auro uestes* (garments with gold embroidered) which also had echoes in Avienus, *Perieg.* 1258; cf. Pru-

dentius, *Steph.* 14.104, *illusa pictæ uestis inania* (embroidered vanities of a pictured garment).

41-56: *Fairness contrasts with Fortune, moving straight, and Simpleness overcomes doubt.*

57-68: *De Tournon holds to Simpleness, enjoys the company of other values, such as Modesty, Trust and Silence, Law and Truth.*

58. **Italy**: a point of pride for Casa (cf. *CL* VI.68); greater autonomy for Italy and especially Florence was to be his final, ill-fated political project when he returned from literary retirement to Rome.

62-63. The theme of whiteness, filth washed away, repeatedly returns, haunting Casa: cf. v. 2.

69-87: *by their help he was able to restore and refurbish Peace.*

78-79. **saved and steadied towns**: how many readers would recall that De Tournon had ordered the destruction of some twenty Waldensian villages in France?

87-92: *Muse, withdraw, there are reasons not to tell all.*

87-88. Melpomene, whom Casa invoked in opening now gets called off for closure: cf. other ring structures at *CL* VII.38-40 and VI.57 with notes. Casa's closing gesture of demurral, in the wake of so much ambitious public utterance, recalls Horace in the third Roman Ode, sounding retreat after an ambitious flight (*Carm.* III.3.69-72). The proliferation of topics of demurral takes on particular irony in the light of Casa's complaint that this poem had been forced out of him by his patron (Introduction, part II). The poem hides, yet brings to the fore, opposites and contradictions: the emphasis on settling citizens for a man who extirpated villages, the claim of a muse unbought in a poem exacted by a patron, and the boast of Italy redeemed when a diplomatic tour-de-force had bullied and bamboozled the pope into renouncing claims to territory usurped by ruthless and self-serving arrogance.

CL X

Genre: lyric.
Meter: Phalaecean or hendecasyllable [see Introduction, part IV].
Literary linkage: Catullus.

Synopsis: Poetics takes over as the theme. Casa speaks with scorn of versifiers who smear many sheets and fill whole books: like the crowd, they misprize the example of Horace, who spurned such facile fullness. The literary point parallels Casa's insistence on moderation as a moral creed, yet the application is new. Moderation, which was an ethical motive for Casa's retreat into writing, returns as an aesthetic principle that requires a retreat from writing, specifically from filling a book too full. This is the first hint that Casa thinks of these poems as a single book. The very concept of a book entails regard for structure, not only beginning and unfolding, but winding down.

Comment

To speak about his engagement with Horace, Casa goes outside the range of Horatian meter and language. He professes his Horatian poetics of measure and timely closure in a meter—the hendecasyllable or Phalaecean—and in a literary terminology that recall Catullus and his Renaissance followers, among them notably the same Flaminio whose ghost was summoned to open the book. The use of Catullan means to affirm Horatian ends fits the pattern of literary demurral (*recusatio*), in which a poet excuses himself from writing in some other genre but in the course of begging off produces a sample of what it is he refuses to do. So Casa, giving voice to the Horatian aesthetic he has been developing, does so in the kind of Catullan pastiche that Flaminio and others turned out with astonishing facility. They filled whole books that lacked Casa's tightly calculated structure of variation and progression. His statement in their style stands apart from the Horatian scheme that it confirms, as does the elegy at the start.

Notes

1–4: there are those whose pretty verses smear huge quantities of paper.
1. **Some with verselet:** *Sunt qui versiculo* recalls a famous verse of Horace, *Sunt quos curriculo* (Some with chariot), at *Carm* I.1.3–4, only to to make a pointed departure. Horace contrasted such ambitions as chariot racing, greed, and politics with his own measured poetic life, a contrast appropriated by Casa in *CL* I, II, III, VI, and VIII. But now Casa posits a similar contrast in poetics, adapting the traditional catalogue of contrasting values (priamel), for which see W. H. Race, *The Classical Priamel from Homer to Boethius* (Leiden: Brill, 1982).
    versiculus: the diminutive of verse, belongs to a vocabulary of

poetic self-irony (cf. already *CL* III.17), a self-deprecating voice familiar from Horatian epode and satire (*Epod.* 11.2; *Serm.* I.2.109, 10.32, 58) and from Catullus (16.3, 6; 50.4)

rather slender: *minutiore* recalls Catullus's *minuta magno* (tiny great), which was an ironical antitheton with alliteration (*Carm.* 25.12). From here on, Catullan colors predominate: the alliterative and intensified epithets for poetry, *pernitido* and *perfluenti*, the talk of bookrolls dirtied with too voluble verse, the aesthetic preference for slight over long, all smack of Catullus's literary criticism.

5–9: they are like spiders' tiny mouths spinning huge webs.

7–8. **tiny ... long** paradox that slight style can produce excess, which the rest of this verse and the next define as overstuffed poetry books.

8–9. **fill booklets | whole**: *compleant libellos | totos* gains emphasis by postponing the adjective to the next verse (enjambment). The diminutive *libellus* was Catullus's ironical way of introducing his own book in *Carm.* 1.1. The concept of the poetry book and its aesthetics thus surfaces in Casa, inviting readers to consider how the present group of poems form a book and justifying its short length.

9. **verselet rather slender**: returns to initial motif at midpoint in the fashion of Catullan structure.

10–16: whether they count as bards, let the crowd decide, and poets like the crowd who do not prize Horace, since he scorned writing too much.

10–11. **bards ... | crowd**: juxtaposing *uatum* and *uulgus*, Casa contrasts the weightier name of poet, which he appropriated from Horace and Virgil at the peak of his pride (*CL* IX.9), with his perennial nemesis, portrayed as base in aesthetics, now, as well as ethics (cf. *CL* II.24; III.6; XI.17, 32); cf. Horace's resounding opener to his third book of odes (*Carm* III.1.1): *odi profanum uulgus* (I hate the uninitiate crowd).

13. **muse**: Thalia, muse of comedy, associated by Virgil with the erotic and the simpler, sylvan, mode in pastoral (*Bucolics* 6.2). Previously Casa addressed Melpomene (*CL* VI.2; IX.4, 88), who was associated with tragedy and whom Horace invoked both in the mourning ode (*Carm.* I.24.3), which Casa echoed in *CL* VI, and as the authorizing deity of high lyric (*Carm.* IV.3.1).

Flaccus: only the cognomen of Horace appears in Casa and only here; the name *Horatius* stands for the dead Farnese duke (*CL* XII).

           best of poets: a tag from Catullus on "best" and "worst" poets (*Carm.* 49.6–7).

14.   **verselet rather slender**: returns to the motif of midpoint and opening to obtain closure, as often Catullus (*Carm.* 16.1, 16; cf. 36.1, 20). Continues Casa's penchant for ring structure as in *CL* IX, VII, VI, and before.

16.   **to claim**: *occupare* suggests an ambitious preemptive strike by an inflated, epicizing aesthetics, which Horace spurned. He criticized his predecessor Lucilius for writing two hundred verses before and after meals, muddily, standing on one foot (*Serm.* I.10.50, 60–61). Catullus sneered at the copious crudities of Suffenus (*Carm.* 22), compared Volusius's voluminous verse to soiled toilet paper (*cacata charta*, *Carm.* 36.1, 20), and prized a friend's "small monuments," leaving the people to "delight in swollen Antimachus" (*Carm.* 95.10): an aesthetics ultimately Callimachean.

CL XI

Genre: lyric (ode).
Meter: Alcaic [see Introduction, part IV].
Literary linkage: Horace.
Synopsis: Paradox multiplies. Commanded by his Farnese connection to keep projecting portentous verse across the Alps, Casa responds with still more acute self-doubt. Nostalgically, he imagines that he began in rustic purity—a kind of literary paradise and baptism—only to fall into the political pit of Rome, where he was corrupted by the crowd. The resulting spots, stains, poisons may be so indelible, he says, as to leave him unfit for the task Farnese orders—praising a spotless French royal virgin, Margaret, "gleaming whiter than her namesake pearl." Blaming the anonymous crowd for the fall that makes him unfit to write the requested poem, Casa masks the reality that Farnese influence and his own ambition had pushed him into the curial career from which he fled to Venice. Renewing the connection, Casa remembers his revulsion, even though he cannot resist the inveterate lure of prestige.

Comment

    Resuming his engagement with Horace, Casa shifts into the Alcaic meter of the great public and prophetic cycle, the "Roman Odes," and evokes one of their central themes—the miraculous rural boyhood and poetic initiation that prepared Horace for his role as priest of the Muses (*Carm.* III.4.1-20). Horace followed the vision of his origins with an eloquent praise of Caesar and a stirring, if ominous, mythic narrative. Casa instead proceeds to a lurid account of his fall at Rome, which he makes the pretext for not writing the poem commanded by his patron. In effect, he gives some praise and satisfaction in the process of refusing, which is typical of the rhetoric of demurral. In this, too, he shows mastery of a Horatian lesson.

Notes
1-4: ingrained spots on character do not yield easily even to long efforts at removal.
1. **Habit, how** ... : a concatenation of themes touching Horace's gravest notes, giving a proper signal of the shift to the meter of the "Roman Odes."
5-16: Casa began in purity, represented by pastoral setting and muses, but Rome corrupted him.
5-7. **springs ... shade ... quiet ... boyhood**: again the poet's origins colored with traditional themes of pastoral myth: cf. *CL* IX.10, VI.61-63, and Horace's *Carm.* III.4.1-20.
8. **Italian muses**: *Aoniæ ... Camœnæ*, again combining Greek with Italic authority as in *CL* III.95-96: in Aonia stands Mt. Helicon, where the Muses bathed in springs and initiated the poet Hesiod (see *Theogony* 1-103). Neo-Latin poets like to imagine themselves dipped in the waters—a literary equivalent of baptism. Casa again speaks of the Italian *Camenae* in keeping with his local pride and following that of Horace, who also combined Greek and Italic—both the muse *Calliope* and the *Camenae* (*Carm.* III.4.2 and 21).
15. **Muse**: again *Thalia*: cf. *CL* X.12 for discussion; her Virgilian association with pastoral suits Casa's emphasis on the contrast between his origin, again represented with pastoral mythemes such as a paradise, and his fall due to urban corruption.
17-25: the crowd seduces and spreads corruption, which time does not suffice to clean.
17. **Vulgar people**: again blaming the crowd, cf. *CL* X.11; II.21 etc.
18. **sly seductions**: literally, Casa says the crowd is apt "to turn minds with Colchian poisons," which implies the princess of Colchis, Medea, and her legendary use of witchcraft to aid, then punish, her lover Jason.

19. **black for white**: this symbolic dichotomy is so absolutely ingrained in Casa's mind that it produces related clusters: the white, clean, well-washed, pure, virgin muses versus everything in some way spotted, dim, corrupted.

25–32: a royal girl merits praise from a white page and uncorrupted lip.

27. **Farnese**: Cardinal Alessandro, the patron whose insistence on this ode Casa documents in his letter to Vettori on 15 July 1553 (see Appendix II, 1553.vii.15, and Introduction, part II).

28. **pearl**: Casa refers obliquely to the "eastern berry," leaving his reader to infer that by this he means *margarita* (pearl) in Greek, hence a learned pun on the name of the recipient of the poem.

31. **against the crowd outside**: closure with another echo of the resonant opening of the "Roman Odes," where *profanum uulgus* literally meant "crowd outside the shrine" (*Carm.* III.1.1). Another defining scene in Casa's ethical and poetic ecology: keep the clean water of poetry for the few.

33–36: Prayer that his complaint be forgotten and his fall washed away.

36. **stain**: *labem* is as close as Casa comes to verbally identifying his personal plight with the concept of orginal sin and the loss of Paradise. He maintains a secular posture in the Latin poems (cf. "Elysian Fields" in *CL* I.2 and note), although not in the *Rime*.

CL XII

Genre: lyric (ode).
Meter: Alcaic [see Introduction, part VI].
Literary linkage: Horace.
Synopsis: Still gripped by the world of ambition, Casa shows resolve and brilliance when his Farnese linkage offers a better theme: the death in battle of young Duke Orazio. He shows no further sign of uncertainty about an ambitious scope as he encompasses history and heroic action. In closing he hails the Farnese house as the "light of Italy and Latium," continuing to endow these places with the mythic aura assigned them in the ninth poem, no longer using them as a pretext to justify retirement in Venice.

Comment

Casa could hardly have expected the death of Orazio Farnese, but when the occasion arose, he made sure that the resulting ode would fit the scheme of his book. The new ode complements its predecessor in three ways: the meter again Alcaic, again an address to a French royal princess, and finally reference again to Farnese power. The two odes form a pair that coheres not only through similarity but through significant difference, with variants explored and exhausted in the complementary opposites counterposed. Casa's concluding praise of the family is so emphatic and far-reaching that it sounds less like the climax of just one, even magniloquent, ode than the closing flourish for a book. Structural coherence also gains through the shift in theme from flattery to consolation and from obsessive doubt of self to confident focus on others.

Notes

1–4: we offer mourning where praise was owed.

1. **West**: *Hesperia*, again the Virgilian name for Italy as the land of destiny (cf. *CL* V.38; IX.29 and notes), yet now tinged by Virgilian melancholy at the loss of a young leader, coloring the pride that Casa invests in the Farnese house (cf. "hope of Latium … pride of Italy" in vv. 5, 8 and *CL* IX.58 and VI.68, with apposite notes).

2. **Muse**: again *Thalia*, by now established as the muse for this closing cycle, hence a sign of local coherence in the book (cf. *CL* XI.16 and X.12).

3. **grieving threnody**: *nænia lugubris*, cf. *Munus lugubre Næniam* (grieving gift: Threnody) in *CL* VI.2.

5–9: that sword destroyed the flower of Italy and hopes of Latium.

6. **Latium**: invested by Casa with hints of old Roman tradition (*CL* VI.37 and note), which he associates with Farnese prestige (*CL* V.2 and VIII.22). In Latium, just north of Rome, Castro, the old family seat, and Ronciglione were under the control of Duke Orazio (see below), and Cardinal Alessandro would soon begin erecting his imposing villa at Caprarola nearby (see Coffin, *Villa* 281–84).

9–11: I do not reproach your Mother's vehement lamentation.

9. *Horati*: addressing the duke in the vocative case. Orazio Farnese (1522?–July 18, 1554), younger brother of Cardinal Alessandro and Ottavio, died in Flanders defending Hesdin against imperial forces, who razed it.

12–16: nor would I reproach your young widow; let her mourn.

17–24: you, Diane, should spare nothing in mourning, since your pleasures fell just as they were rising.

17. **royal girl**: the sixteen-year-old Diane of Valois (1538–1619), natural daughter of King Henry II of France by an Italian woman,

married Orazio Farnese six months before he died—one of the latest scenes depicted in the cycle of historical murals at Cardinal Farnese's villa in Caprarola.

18. **hair and cheeks untorn**: the classical rite of female lamentation, hardly current in the French court. Typical of the frequent tension between classical tropes or styles and contemporary reality.

25–32: he died in the thick of the fight.

25–26. **Not forgetting forebears nor your kingly father**: a diplomatic nod to family pride in the grandfather, Pope Paul III (cf. Introduction, part I) and in the widow's father, King Henry II.

33–36: he glories with ancient heroes below.

33–35. Again Casa thinks of pagan afterlife (cf. *CL* I.1–2).

35–36. **Hector, Latin and Italian kings**: assimilates the young duke as a new hero into the fabric of myth inherited from Virgil's *Aeneid*, including the Trojan Hector and the native Latins and Rutulians—honorably defeated forerunners of the Italians: another touch of ideology and pride (cf. vv. 1, 5–8).

37–44: Glory, assure the fame of Orazio and the Farnese line.

37. **Grecian Muses**: interprets "Thespian sisters," so called from Thespiae, a town in Boeotia below the Muses' mountain Helicon (cf. *CL* XI.8).

41. **muses hymning many praises**: for *Musis & Polyhymnia*, spelling out the Greek etymology of the latter (many hymns), who is a muse invoked by Horace in the programmatic ode (*Carm.* I.1.33) that has been a subtext (cf. *CL* VIII and X).

42. **hand along ... to keep**: *trade* echoes and reverses the prayer to the muses, *tradite* (hand over to oblivion,) which was Casa's outburst of despair (*CL* XI.34). The echo and reversal add to the evidence for attention to coherence in the book.

44. **Italy's ... Latium's**: the geographical grounds of Farnese myth are evoked again in a final burst of pride (cf. vv. 6, 8, and notes; also the Italic heroes at vv. 35–36).

CL XIII

Genre: lyric (ode).
Meter: Asclepiad [type 5, see Introduction, part III].
Literary linkage: Horace.

Synopsis: Debt of praise long owed a scholar-friend, whose wealth of learning enriches all Tuscany, and who is not seduced by ambition.

Comment

From his excursion into high themes, Casa returns to literature and Florence, with which he began the exile poems in *CL* VI. Adopting a financial metaphor, he announces a literary debt so great that his Muse is too poor to pay. He further magnifies his creditor, making a kind of payment on the debt, by describing him metaphorically as a husbandman who enriches the Tuscan people with crops of genius, a legendary mentor, never corrupted by the infection of the crowd or shaken by ambition—in short, the "light" of their "celebrated fatherland."

In directing this foison of compliments to his friend and future editor Pier Vettori, Casa brings together and amplifies leading themes from earlier in the book. He recalls the ethical and aesthetic ideals praised in the Venetian Bembo (*CL* III) and Florentine Ubaldino (*CL* III and VI). These are the values that he sought to practice and keep secure also in the first poems of the retreat (*CL* VII and VIII) before his climb to French and Farnese themes.

Coming back now, he perceives his whole retreat differently. In prospect it offered hope of escaping from a corrupt society to one ideally governed (*CL* II and V). As he imagined the story, retreat was to be the physical premise for moral redemption, which he would achieve through the "busy leisure" of literary life, free of ambitious influences. Now, looking back and taking stock, Casa describes the retreat less positively as an "exile in harsh hills." But exile in ancient Rome was a bitter symptom of the breakdown of the Republic, associated by Cicero and Virgil with the loss of civic status, impoverishment, danger, discomfort, humiliation, and emotional stress, often death. Quintessentially, as in the case of Ovid, it implied longing to get back to Rome. The negative overtones suggest that, in Casa's eyes, his remedy for moral failing has come to seem extreme. His reference to the hills as harsh also signals a shift: when setting out, he focused on the polity of Venice (*CL* V); now he emphasizes the roughness of his rural retreat, approaching the urban viewpoint of the elegy (*CL* I), which spoke of the poverty of the hills.

To be sure, the country, among woods and springs, was where he imagined his own pure origins before his fall in Rome (*CL* XI). Calling country rough, Casa steps back from his commitment to the austerities of withdrawal and a humble literary life. He sounds ready to shut up shop and go. The harvest here has been enough, he adds, in a classic sign of closure. Meanwhile, he has been dropping hints of alternative values and styles. He has praised Vettori as the "light of my much celebrated fatherland" and the Farnesi as "light of Latium": his admiration and aspiration flit from the humble northern hills towards Florence and above all Rome. He has come full circle, back to the position with which he began the book: only there he was in the city and speaking of its need for advice from the country; now speaking from the country, he sounds ready to go back to advise the city himself.

In the book's unfolding, the pair of poems (*CL* XI, XII) recalling the "Roman Odes" crowned Casa's emulation of Horace. The only challenge remaining was to withdraw in ways that would continue and enhance the Horatian appropriation. Casa used one remarkable technique of closure at the end of the Asclepiadean cycle (*CL* IX), when he returned to the metrical type of the opening poem (*CL* VI). Now, to close the entire lyric cycle he again uses links to its beginning. In theme, this praise of a living Florentine humanist complements the praise of the deceased Florentine humanist. In meter, Casa returns to the Asclepiadean family of the first four odes and selects yet another type—the fifth—again sensitive to how meter demarcates structure in the Horatian book. Horace used the fifth Asclepiad as rarely as the first—only three times; most evidently in the first book (*Carm.* I.11) it capped the opening cycle—the so-called "Parade" of ten different meters (*Carm.* I.1-11). Casa's own sample closes and caps his lyric cycle. It is a measure of the weight assigned to this final ode that Casa changes to a third muse, neither returning to Melpomene, who opened and closed his first lyric cycle (*CL* VI and IX), nor continuing with Thalia (*CL* X, XI, XII), but moving on to a higher muse (see note, v. 1).

Notes
1-2: praise owed now for a long time, a debt.
1. **Calliope**: muse of epic, invoked by Horace to descend and validate his autobiographical myth (*Carm.* III.4.1); for Casa a closing shift upwards from the muses of the lyric cycles.
2. **promissory note**: metaphorical expression of literary debt in accounting terms, like two Florentine businessmen.

3-11: the praise must be generous, for Phoebus has been generous with him.
6-11. Scholarly riches praised through metaphors of georgic fullness: like fertile farms that feed their towns, Vettori feeds the Tuscans.

11-14: likewise the Centaur, Chiron, enriched the Greeks with arts.
11-14. Mythic comparison likens Vettori to the teacher of Achilles, Chiron. Casa's language achieves an intricate counterpoint of

sound and sense with compound epithets in epic style: *frondifero semifer* (leaf-bearing half-wild).

14–17: time will never remove the fruits of his scholarship.

14–16. "Sooner will the impossible occur in nature than your books be lost": *adynata* in the manner of classical rhetoric (cf. Virgil, *Bucolics* 1.59–63).

18–24: ambition, that infects the crowd, never got to you, although it traces its origins back to the Titans.

18–20. Closure foreshadowed by recursion and reemphasis: Casa brings back and weaves together motifs from his own book and from Horace: moral disease and the contagion of vulgar taste (*CL* I.15, II.45–48, III.93), ambition to win the race (*Carm.* I.1.3–14; cf. *CL* X.1; II.15, 25, 48; III.45), and the passing onlookers (*Carm.* IV.3.22: *praetereuntium*). Thematically, the result is a ring structure within the book.

19. **ambition**: emphatic denial precisely where suspicion was justified, since the letters document Vettori's courtship of Cardinal Farnese: Casa (Narvesa) to Vettori (Rome), 26 April 1555, (Appendix II, 1555.iv.26) and Annibale Rucellai (Rome) to Vettori (back in Florence), 20 July 1555, (Appendix II, 1555.vii.20 and see Introduction, part II).

21–24. Myth of ambition's origin from the giants that tried to assail heaven told in the most heroic manner of Horatian mythopoeia (e.g., *Carm.* I.3.25–40, III.4.42–80).

25–28: greed and gold never got to you either, washed by the muses, light of my famous land.

28–32: enough this harvest in exile.

28. **enough for me the yield**: a georgic metaphor for the closure of Casa's literary retirement and his book. "Enough" (*sat, satis*) was a crucial motif of measure and closure in Virgil's *Bucolics* (e.g., 1.47, 3.111, 6.24, 10.70).

29. **exile**: the pejorative term for what began as a promise of redeeming and healing retirement (*CL* II.5): a sign that Casa is ready to get back to Rome.

Casa pulls together his themes: a final thrust at the crowd and ambition, vision of sparkling cleanliness through literature, the muse, health, Castalian spring, his native Florence prized. Poetry in metaphor becomes yield, both grain and interest. The rejected world of gain comes back as a metaphor for literary redemption. "Lazy exile" echoes literary leisure (the *desidia* of *CL* III.15, 44). "Harsh hills" puts a negative color on the lingering idea of pastoral retreat (*CL* I), as does "meager lyre" on the poetics of limitation (*CL* X). Casa posits the paradox of how to be big with his friend in this self-consciously restricted stylistic mode.

CL XIV, XV, *and* XVI

Genre: epigram.
Meter: elegiac couplet [see Introduction, part IV]
Literary linkage: Catullus.
Synopsis: In keeping with his new orientation, Casa suddenly emphasizes an unbearable feature of his rural surroundings. He pleads with nearby bells that, if they will just let him sleep the coming night, he will endow them with new ropes and racks (*CL* XIV). He laments that then only, when lightning, rivers, seas fall still, these bells too will (*CL* XV). He protests that just when storms and rainbows stop, when fish leave seas, shells shores, shade glades, will cease these bells (*CL* XVI).

Comment

Three snappy variations confirm the impression that Casa is ready to abandon his rural retreat and close its story; for the new theme undercuts the ideal premises on which the book was based: restraint in art and life sustained by rural repose. Farewell already radiated from the Horatian meter, theme, and structure of the Vettori ode, even before this rhetorical démarche. Metrically, the three poems represent a return to the basic form of elegiac distichs or couplets with which the book opened, only that these couplets are used in the manner of a different genre. Instead of the lengthier arguments or narratives of elegy, they have the brevity and point of epigram, which, again like elegy and the hendecasyllable of *CL* X, was a form that Catullus and Flaminio, but never Horace, used.

The epigrams also parallel the hendecasyllable in theme and function with their talk of excessive fluency and failure to close even while they close. The hendecasyllable departed from Horatian structure to assert a Horatian regime. So, too, the epigrams speak of failed closure yet enclose the whole book in a single structure, which goes beyond Horatian moderation and meter into genres and themes that bode a return to the city.

Notes

CL XIV: *the poet offers new rope and scaffolding if the bells will give him*

a little respite—in the form of a vow, quid pro quo, a virtuoso display of mock persuasion and onomatopoetic skill.
CL XV: *When nature's noises still, so will these bells.*

Tacitly admitting the futility of the vow, Casa makes three variations, each occupying one couplet, on the theme of impetuous and never-stopping natural noise (*adynata*: cf. the "impossibility" trope, *CL* XIII.16–17 and note; also the marked alliterative effects).

3–4. Flooding rivers evoked by plosive sonority and virtuoso positioning of noun-modifier pairs, which are indicated by underlining, bold-face, and bold-face underlined:

Cum <u>sueta</u> in Pontum **plenis** decurrere **ripis**
  <u>**praecipitem**</u> sistent <u>flumina</u> prona **<u>pedem</u>**

Cf. the similar stylemes in Catullus (*Carm.* 65.5–6)

namque <u>mei</u> nuper **lethaeo gurgite** <u>fratris</u>
  Pallidulum manans alluit <u>unda</u> **<u>pedem</u>**.

CL XVI: *When noises, rainbow shades, and nature's denizens desert, then too these bells—varies and amplifies the "impossibility" trope.*

1–2. Three noises, the entire range of *CL* XV, compressed into one couplet.

3–4. Two colors "forsake" the rainbow, which is evoked by mythological indirection as "Thaumas' cloud-born child," i.e., Iris.

5–6. Three denizens will abandon their habitats, where "shade" stands by metonymy for what makes it—the leaves of the trees.

7. **sweet Cornelius**: a sexton? a patron from the noble Venetian family Corner? Catullus at the beginning of his book greeted *Cornelius*, whom he identified as the producer of a work more grave and vast than his own trifles (*Carm.* 1.3).

Bells enter Casa's correspondence only in a brief complaint towards the end of his retreat: Casa (Narvesa) to Vettori (Florence), 23 January 1555 (Appendix II, 1555.i.23; and see Introduction, part II). The ruins of the abbey of Narvesa, which was destroyed during the Battle of the Piave,[1] look eastward down from the Montello to where a tall and slender belfry, of later date, rises next to the "Via Monsignor Della Casa." The marginal irritant in life becomes an occasion for this paradoxical and virtuoso finish to the book.

---

[1] 1917–1918: commemorated by the inscription on a spare cross near the ruined abbey, "Qui sul Montello l'onda nemica s'infranse" (Here on the Montello the enemy wave broke).

POSTSCRIPT

Following the editorial dispute echoed in Casa's letters (Appendix II, 1548.i.28 and 1548.ix.29), the posthumous edition of Bembo's poems finally appeared: *Delle Rime di M. Pietro Bembo Terza Impressione* (Valerio Dorico and Luigi brothers, October 1548, "ad instantia di M. Carlo Gualteruzzi"). It exemplifies the network of relationships in which Casa thrived.

After the spare title, a letter from Pope Paul III grants apostolic benediction to each and every reader, extolls the culture of Cardinal Bembo, and cites his last will that publication be arranged by Gualteruzzi, who is granted copyright for fifteen years. Next comes a fulsome dedication to the pope's grandson, Casa's patron, the twenty-eight year old Cardinal Alessandro, composed by Annibale Caro at the behest of Bembo's literary executors, Gualteruzzi and Girolamo Quirino (Casa's first host in Venice). Caro goes so far as to suggest that Bembo was a Homer to this Alexander and found in him a better patron than ever Ennius in Scipio or Virgil in Maecenas.

The *canzoniere* proper opens by invoking the Muses of Helicon and introducing the theme of love with Dantesque echoes (p. 1: "Piansi e cantai lo stratio et l'aspra guerra. ... Donna scesa dal ciel uidi passarme") only to close with a series of sonnets addressed to specific persons and culminating in praise for Casa. This final set opens with one sonnet each to TRIPHON Gabriele, Veronica Gambara di Coreggio, and Giorgio Trissino (pp. 96–97: the names capitalized appear so in the texts; the other dedications are pointedly declared in the index of first lines, pp. 153–61). The series continues with three sonnets to Vittoria Colonna, Marchesa di Pescara (including the paronomastic salute, p. 98: "Alta Colonna, et ferma a le tempteste"). One each goes to Bembo's executors CARLO Gualteruzzi and GIROLAMO QUIRINO (p. 99), to Francisco Maria Molza (p. 100, cf. p. 82) whom Casa praised in his salute to Bembo (*CL* III.96), and to Benedetto VARCHI (p. 100, honoring also Florentine culture, exemplified by VETTORIA, the future correspondent and editor of Casa). There follow no less than six sonnets for Lisabetta QUIRINA (pp. 101–3, Casa's hostess in Venice), one for Paolo GIOVIO (p. 104), and two honoring Cardinal Farnese (pp. 104–5: "Signor; poi che fortuna in adornarui" and "Se qual è dentro in me, chi lodar brama"). Next to his patron, then, in the honorific final position comes CASA, his praise of Bembo's virtue (*CL* III) well repaid (p. 105: "CASA; in cui le uirtuti han chiaro albergo;"). Some of these last poems replied to sonnets (by Gambara, Trissino, Colonna, Molza) or provoked replies (from Varchi and Casa), all of which appear later in the volume (pp. 148–52, * [four unnumbered pages]).

Before the climactic parade, one sonnet praises the pious Giberti (p. 91). Only after and outside the *canzoniere*, in a group on the deaths of Bembo's brother and many other persons (pp. 107–27), does a sonnet evoke Cosimo Geri (p. 119), Casa's one-time correspondent and the victim of Pier Luigi Farnese, whose papal father and cardinal son figure so prominently as patrons framing the book.

In a note to the reader (p. 165), Gualteruzzi states his original intention to give the reader only what Bembo himself gathered and arranged for this end ("vivendo compilò et ordinò a questo fine"), but says that "un gran Signor mio ... con la sua molta auttorità" has imposed the addition of other poems. The only imaginable subject of such terms must be Cardinal Farnese himself.

APPENDIX I

Punctuation Sampler

Since CL VII and CL IX exist in manuscripts from Casa and his secretary, I include a sampler of variant punctuations.

CL VII

3.   Norunt non secus, ac *1564*
    Norunt, non secus ac *AUTOGRAPH, 1563*
10.   excutias, *1563, 1564* (clarifies boundary of clause)
    excutias *AUTOGRAPH*
11.   *vox;* 1564
    uox: *1563*
    uox, *AUTOGRAPH*
13.   sordido: *1564*
    sordido; *1563*
    sordido, *AUTOGRAPH*
21.   , uera ubi concinunt, *1564, 1563*
    uera ubi concinunt *AUTOGRAPH*
22.   solent: nec *1564*
    solent. nec *1563*
    solent. Nec *AUTOGRAPH*
24.   Spernit psallere tibiae,
      Sic virtus, populus si taceat, sedens
      Cessabit: nihilo nec *1564*
    Nescit psallere tibiae.
      Sic uirtus; populus si taceat sedens;
      Cessabit, nihilo quae *1563*
    Nescit psallere tibiae.
      Sic uirtus populus si taceat sedens
      Cessabit, nihilo quae *AUTOGRAPH*

	CL IX
1564]	ROME.
20. diu.]	diu
21. ueluti,]	ueluti
22. dumis]	dumis,
27. hostis,]	hostis;
33. Fortunae,]	Fortunae;
50. exitu,]	exitu;
53. Nudans.]	Nudans:
60. Natorum,]	Natorum
62. sordibus,]	sordibus;

The latter sets off the first two members of a tricolon from the third; the former sets the parallel members at one and the same level.

64. Arcanum insequitur,]	Arcanum, insequitur:
66. Districto]	Districto,
68. pallio.]	pallio:
73. Pacem,]	Pacem;
84. Torpens]	Torpens,

forces careful consideration of structure: *torpens* ... *timor* forms an emphatic pair embracing the predicate, which likewise forms a sub-unit of sound and sense: *quam peperit* ... *pacem*.

85. Pacem,]	Pacem;

APPENDIX II

Selected Letters

Casa's letters talk of trade in verses admired or rebuked, of young men's worries about better jobs or housing on tight budgets, and later of the intrigues of diplomacy and the comedy of manners when he was beseiged in Venice by competing agents, a hostile theologian, and a brilliant, beautiful woman. The death of Casa's patron, Pope Paul III, brings modulation and release: the rural retreat in hope to write.

A resolve to write letters in Latin won praise for a friend from Casa.[1] His own were sought by Pier Vettori for his edition of Casa's Latin works.[2] Casa's heir gave low priority to the request. His eventual reply disappoints the would-be editor but documents some mechanisms and material constraints of the genre: a few letters there are, writes Casa's nephew Rucellai, but not such as could be published; for others it is doubtful whether registers were kept, and the copies must be lost; they might be stored in some old boxes, hard to get at:[3] this more than two years after Vettori's first request and scarcely two months before the book appeared in print in early June. Better destiny was reserved for numerous other letters, which were hoarded in the cupboards of noble families and published in compendious editions with the rest of Casa's writings in the eighteenth century.[4] Others still are being collected and published;[5] many, especially diplomatic correspondence, remain scattered in libraries and archives.

---

[1] Letter of 1535.vii.03 below. In reporting dates I have adopted a uniform system that makes it easy for the reader to index and search: YEAR.month.DAY.

[2] Letter from Annibale Rucellai: 1561.ix.06 below.

[3] Letter from Annibale Rucellai in Rome: 1564.iii.24, below.

[4] Florence, 1707; Venice, 1728; Naples, 1733; Venice, 1752; then only the Italian, Milan, 1806.

[5] For example, Santosuosso, "Inediti casiani" and "Le opere italiane"; O. Moroni, *Carlo Gualteruzzi* (Vatican City, 1984), 198.

Here I have selected only a few letters and parts of letters to document Casa's literary activity before, around, and after the *Carminum Liber*. Occasionally, I have summarized material that illustrates his relations with the wider contexts in which he moved.[6] For texts, I have relied on the several collectors and editors.[7] The older editors were not always consistent in reporting forms of address and salutations. What formulas they give I have printed, adopting their typographical convention of italics, which set off and underline the formulaic language. Precisely because the formularies now seem stylized and stereotyped, they serve as a useful reminder of some of the rules of the game played by Casa and his friends. The elaborate salutations mirror the manners and social codes that Casa reflected, too, in his treatises—the Latin *Reciprocal Duties between Weaker and More Powerful Friends* and the more famous *Galateo* in Italian. In the salutations, varying dosages of compliment signal changing attitudes and degrees of rank, which shift through time, as the roles and fortunes of correspondents alter and even get exchanged: when no longer "Ambassador," Casa still signs "Archbishop" to a friend for whom he had once been plain "Your Gio"; his nephew can sign "Of Your Lordship Servant and Most Obedient Son" at the moment when he becomes most demanding and pretentious.

1532.xi.14: Casa (Rome) to Beccadelli (Fano):[8]
A M. Lodovico Beccatello.
... Avete veduto del Mondo, così fate mentre che si può, che io ci veggo un dì a Predalbino a piangere i nostri peccati, con più dolcezza che non abbiamo sentita in commetterli, benchè voi non avete grave la coscienza forse come ho io, ne mi sosterrete ch'io parli così in plurale. ...

Gio. vostro

---

[6] This limited agenda excludes the fascinating further evidence of how men of wit and learning maneuvered to survive and sometimes prosper on the margins of ecclesiastical and secular courts. The humanist secretaries, tutors, scholars, always poets cannot compete with popes and kings, cardinals, dukes, and condottieri in the indices to encyclopedias. Justice to their vivacity would require more books.

[7] In the case of damage to the text, I indicate my restoration in angle brackets, the nature of the damage in square brackets as follows: l'adula‹zione› [burned].

[8] *Opere* (1806) 4:339.

1532.xi.24: Casa (Rome) to Geri (Fano):[9]
A Mons. Cosimo Gerio Vescovo di Fano.
... Non voglio che V. S. mi ami più sì di core, come ha fatto fin qui, perchè non lo merito più, come ch'io nol meritava ancora prima: ma ora ch'io ho messo in non cale ogni pensiero, e che una donna *dulcibus illa quidem illecebris*,[10] mi ha tanto mutato, sono indegno che V. S. mi abbia si caro, com'io conosco che mi ha: se io tornerò mai *ad sanitatem*, allora mi amerete: in questo mezzo *vota faciemus, optabimusque nobis mentem meliorem duri*, quando per consiglio e per ajuto umano sono disperato e perduto. ...

Gio. servo di V. S.

1534.viii.07: Casa (Rome) to Beccadelli (Bologna):[11]
A M. Lodovico Beccatelli.
... v'attendo amendui per ogni conto con desiderio: e massimamente per dirizzare la vita mia con la vostra regola, la qual mia vita troverete torta dietro alle sirene del Mondo sopra quello che voi non avreste per avventura stimato poter essere, guardando al viaggio suo passato. State sani. ...

Gio. vostro

1535.iii.11: Casa (Rome) to Geri (Padua):[12]
Molto Rev. Sig. mio Osserv.
... l'uno ha divulgato i miei amori, e fattoli immensi ed incomprensibili; e l'altro ha scritto de'miei versi al Priuli, acciò che siano aspettati perchè la cosa è bella. ...

Gio. servo

1535.vii.03: Casa (Rome) to Beccadelli (Bologna):[13]
A M. Lodovico Beccatello.
... Che voi siete tornato a scrivermi latino, e vogliate usar quella lingua per innanzi, mi piace, e più ancora che abbiate scritto molto ben latino, come, s'io non m'inganno: *quid voveat dulci nutricula maius alumno, quam sapere, et fari possit quae sentiat?*[14] ...

---

[9] *Opere*, 4:341.
[10] Virgil, *Georgics* 3.217, of the cow that makes the bull forget to graze.
[11] *Opere* (1806) 4:349.
[12] *Opere* (1806) 4:350.
[13] *Opere* (1806) 4:352–53.
[14] Horace, *Epist.* I.4.8–9.

Resto di mandarvi l'epistola in versi latini, perchè io non mi son potuto difendere di non esser scuretto, e se io la mandassi di mia mano fra il male scrivere e lo scuro dire v'affaticheria: senza che mi soddisfa malissimo da dovero; pure io la farò scrivere, e manderolla, acciò che non pensiate ch'io voglia che la mia ignoranza ed inezia sia più nota a me stesso che a voi: avrò ben caro che non esca del cerchio vostro, del quale io non cavo M. Flaminio, perchè voglio e piacemi che vi sia; e non vel pongo perchè vi è; lo saluto, e gli desidero felicissime notti e spesse, poichè le sono ora corte, invidio voi a lui e lui a voi, e a tutti due M. Lodovico; e Predalbino a tutti e tre. Vi bacio la mano. ...

Serv. Gio.

1535.viii.05: Casa (Rome) to Geri (Bologna: Predalbino):[15]
A Mons. Cosimo Gerio, Vescovo di Fano.

Quanto maggior pratica ha V. S. nelle epistole di Orazio, tanto meno le dovria piacere la mia, *serio hercle dico*; ma quanto al *jurgatur* mi parea aver detto *jurgamur*, nè con tutto ciò mi piacea, parendomi che si mutasse la persona senza alcuna grazia e fuori di proposito: per avventura saria manco male: *Et patrui verbis objurgat acerbi*.[16] Certo è ch'io non crederei che si usasse *jurgatur* in attiva significazione. *Pacem bellis ubi miscuit atris* a V. S. dispiace, ed a me parea aver fatto una botta a mio modo:[17] tanto sono discosto da saper quel ch'io mi cicali. Pareami aver inserito uno apologo d'Esopo in brevi parole secondo l'usanza d'Orazio, il quale Esopo mette, che un buon vecchio pescando turbava l'acqua ogni dì; e alla vicinanza, che di ciò si dolea, rispose che se esso non avesse intorbidata loro l'acqua, non avria avuto del pane per se; ed è la interpretazione questa stessa, cioè che chi governava in quei tempi metteva sotto sopra e intorbidava la Città per poter camuffare da vivere: e non so s'io mel sognai, che Aristofane usurpa questa novella esso ancora: e credea d'aver risposto a una proposta di sopra, dove dice *bellorum causas jussus praecidere nutris*.[18] Ma pure io ho torto dello *hanc vi-*

---

[15] *Opere* (1806) 4:354–56: Casa discusses the Latin verse epistle promised in 1535.vii.03 above.

[16] *CL* III.21: the phraseology invented here eventually finds its way into the printed edition, identified and labeled as *1564* in the Introduction, part IV.

[17] *CL* III.53: Casa replaced *atris* with *idem 1564*.

[18] *CL* III.43 *1564*.

tam;[19] potrei cicalare un pezzo e pur aver torto. *Enormique decor*,[20] etc. volea dire: *Ineptum anorme*, così com'io avea detto *decor concinnus*; ed era stato avvertito di non so che sopra ciò, ma non d'oscurità alcuna; ed intendeva *anormi* per cosa senza alcuna regola, nè analogia. Se io volessi ora entrarvi 'n un *mare magnum* di dirvi, che vi son servitorissimo perchè mi avete scritto alla libera, e ancora quali sono le ragioni, perch'io dico male di quei versi; vi farei venir voglia di pregare quanti santi ci avete nella Chiesiola fino a quello che si tiene il capo in mano, che non mi venisse più voglia di comporre e commentare: basta ch'io vi ho a fare una frotta d'inchini, el'impatterò a Pandolfo. Attenderò a fare de'Capitoli, che con manco fatica riescano meglio, e s'imparano ed allegansi. ...

Serv. Gio.

1536.ii.04: Casa (Rome) to Geri (Padua):[21]
Molto Rev. Sig. mio.

Bisogneria che io scrivessi alcuna cosa dello epigramma, volendo rispondere a tutte le parti della lettera di V. S., ed io non mi ricordo ora così bene il verso che mi spiaceva, ancora che tutto non mi piaceva: e sono lungi dalle Muse questo anno molto bene, nè mi dispiace, perciò che erano moleste a me ed agli altri: voi mi lodate sempre assai, e se è per quella ragione, per la quale tutte le nostre cose piacciano a noi medesimi, ho caro, e mi è di molto contento d'essere quasi in quella medesima ragione, dove V. S. conta se medesimo, e che essa sia φίλαυτος nelle mie cose: ma se voi mi dessi la baja, saria ben chiaro della filosfia, e quasi ancora della ipocrisia, la quale non vi lasciate imporre, e non ve ne vestite, acciò che possiate dire essere senza vizio, che se non avete questo, certo siate: benchè sendo buono, come si dice per M. Lodovico nostro, non credo che possiate essere capace d'ipocrisia, se essa è simulazione di essere quello che altri non è. Ma forse che io farei meglio ad esser pur poeta ben magro, come io soglio, che andar filosofando con V. S., ancor ch'io sia alle mani con l'Etica, come vi deve aver scritto il soprannominato Beccatello.

---

[19] *CL* III.46: *vitam hanc 1564* required by prosody.
[20] *CL* III.39: *anormi 1564*.
[21] *Opere* (1806) 4:356–58.

> Quintia Romana meretrix bene cognita plebi,
>   Haec, quam custodem fornicis esse ferunt,
> In quam profestis nautae, festisque diebus
>   Exercet validum rustica turba latus;
> Dispeream Salio possit collata videri.
>   Ni proba, nique Ithaci conjuge casta magis.
> Quin ultro haec puero concedit, et ut videt una
>   Tot cupidis illum nocte patere viris;
> "Hunc lectum, hanc" ait "exiguo cum lumine sellam
>   Arma meae melior tu, puer, artis, habe."[22]

Mi dispiace meno come io ve lo mandai l'altra volta, e poi che vi piace che io vi scriva de'versi, vi ho voluto mandar questi, e credo che ve ne parrà quello che ne ho detto io, che gli altri sono men tristi.

V. S. vuol pur che Mons. Bembo sappia tutte le mie sciocchezze, poichè mostraste a S. S. la lettera, ch'io scrivea a Pier Antonio almeno quando V. S. ne avrà occasione, facciagli fede, quanto io ho sempre conosciuto e adorato il suo divino ingegno, l'altre eccellenze sue, acciò che S. S. possa conoscere da questo, ch'io non son sempre sciocco nè pazzo. ...

1536.iii.02: Casa (Rome) to Geri (Padua):[23]
Molto Rev. Sig. mio Osserv.

Venne il Priuli, al quale farei voluntieri come V. S. desidera, carezze e comodo quanto io potessi per amendue i conti che scrivete: ma non ardisco invitarlo, che mi pare tanto dato allo spirito, e io sono, come sa V. S., poco divoto, e vivo alla libera, nè posso così al primo lasciar questa lunga usanza mia: come che per quanto intendo, esso e M. Galeazzo non sono però disperati dell'anima mia, studiando io l'Etica, la quale nondimeno ha fatto poco frutto in me, tanto che io ne ho letto alcuna volta di buon pezzi in un certo loco, che io dirò poi a V. S. quando saremo a Predalbino; basta che avresti riso a vedermi andar su per un tetto con l'Etica sfortunata sotto il braccio: e perchè V. S. sappia il poco frutto di quel libro velio, ve ne dirò un'altra, non senza versi, acciò che non siano lette le mie lettere.

---

[22] For a translation of the Latin, see Introduction, part II.
[23] *Opere* (1806) 4:359–61.

Ci è una gentil donna forestiera, con la quale M. M. Antonio Soranzo ha per alcuni suoi affari molta domestichezza, ed essa è molto gentil persona, ed in versi fa il diavolo. A costei accadde scriver a questi giorni una polizza al Soranzo, e poi la richiedea con molta instanza, e volea la sua polizza a tutti partiti del mondo: io pregai il Soranzo, che le dicesse che un suo compagno glie l'avesse tolta, e la tenesse per molta affezione che portava alla donna molto cara, e la pregasse che gliela donassi, e se essa volea saper qual fosse il suo amico, dicesse che era io, e'così fece: ma non di meno ella volea pure la polizza sua, pregando e lui e me che ci contetassimo diד restituirla, perchè era scritto in essa alcune parole che poteano esser intese contro alla buona fama sua: ora non si potendo più negarla, feci che il Soranzo scrisse questi versi pur sulla medesima carta, e che gliela rendesse: e perchè io mi descrivo in essi con alcune qualità non mie, acciò che V. S. mi riconosca, intenda me per il dolce amico; e 'l Soranzo è il Poeta; e quello che scrive i versi.

> Il dolce amico mio fin qui si franco
> Che cader non porria per colpo leve,
> Novellamento a voi, donna, si rende:
> E con le spalle e'l cor non vinto unquanco
> Se non da voi pur ora il giogo prende.
> E certo se virtù prezzar si deve,
> Se vera fè locar quanto altri crede,
> È non indegno servo di mercede.

Certo l'Etica non mi devria avere insegnato nè questa incontinenza, *neque tam impudentem* ἀλαζονείαν; nè voglio dir ora a V. S. chi ha più operato verso il fine suo, l'Etica, o questi versi, lo dirò poi pure a Predalbino: la quale solitudine ed ozio mi sta nel core e nell'anima molto spesso, e se lo stato mio non pendesse tanto dalla fortuna, prometterei a V. S. un decennio, anzi cominceria a contarlo dal XXXVI. ora non ho che promettere altro che io desidero sommamente.

Se io credessi che V. S. avesse pensiero o dubbio che le sue lettere non mi fossero carissime, sarei tutto infaccendato a persuadervi, che io le desidero molto più che tutte le altre lettere, se fossero bene di chi mi ajutò a studiar l'Etica, poichè io ho preso a far l'adultero in questa lettera: ma so che non ne dubitate, ma scrivete così per farmi paura. ....
Gio.

1542.iv.07: Casa (Rome) to Beccadelli (Bologna):[24]
Mag. M. Lodovico.

    Annibale Rucellai mio nipote, del quale vi parlai alla vostra partita di qua lungamente viene a Bologna, com'io vi dissi, in casa M. Lorenzo Bianchetti, dove io son sicuro che starà bene e comodamente per la bontà di quelli gentiluomini tanto amorevoli e cortesi, ma bisogna che voi ancora pigliate parte di questo peso, anzi la principal parte che è di provvedergli d'uno maestro, che stia con esso lui nella casa medesima di M. Lorenzo, ed abbia cura di lui così nelle lettere come nei costumi, nei quali è alquanto trascorso, come ancora vi dissi: e vuol essere persona severa, perchè il putto è poco usato ad alcuna obbedienza; e bene di buonissimo ingegno e di spirito grande, tal che se si può volgerlo agli studj e frenarlo un poco, spero che fia di molto contento a suo padre e a me che non lo amo manco che figluolo. ...

                                           Gio. della Casa.

1544.ix.20: Casa (Venice, as ambassador of the Pope) to Gualteruzzi (Rome, as secretary of Cardinal Farnese):[25]
Magn. M. Carlo.

    Sono arrivato sano, Dio grazie, e sbrigatomi delle cerimonie pubbliche, pur secondo il mio costume arido e salvatico. ...

    Mi pare mill'anni che Mons. Reverendissimo Bembo pigli il possesso, e sapere che V. S. Reverendissima si tenga bene accomodata, come mi tengo io del Quirini, dico del maschio, che la femmina non ho veduta ancora; e M. Flaminio mezzo mezzo m'impedisce sotto spezie di carità, ricordando con quanta onestà e gravità convenga stare un Legato, e che non ista bene a tor l'innamorata al prossimo. Ma io non son per credergli nè l'un nè l'altro.

                                           Il Legato di Venezia.

1545.i.15: Casa (Venice, as ambassador of the Pope) to Gualteruzzi (Rome, as secretary of Cardinal Farnese):[26]
Magn. M. Carlo.

    ... I versi non saranno veduti se non dal Cardinale e da M. Fla-

---

[24] *Opere* (1806) 4:363.
[25] *Opere* (1806) 4:178.
[26] *Opere* (1806) 4:198.

minio, che può ben dire Sua Signoria ancora quella canzona, con tutto che si faccia di buona villa: così Sua Signoria Reverendissima imparerà a stuzzicare il formicajo, e mi perdonerà gli errori che vi sono, dicendomeli però: e a voi piacerà baciare le mani di Sua Signoria Reverendissima a mio nome.

Gio. vostro.

1545.ii.05: Casa (Venice, as ambassador of the Pope) to Gualteruzzi (Rome, as secretary of Cardinal Farnese):[27]
Magn. M. Carlo.
... Madonna Isabetta mi tolse jeri sera la canzone, e così non la posso mandare a voi, ma credo bene che la vedrete; e mi raccomando per amore di Dio che non la vegga se non voi, miei Signori.

Gio. vostro.

1545.iv.18: Casa (Venice, as ambassador of the Pope) to Beccadelli (Trent, as Secretary to the Council):[28]
Rev. M. Lodovico.
No si giocarà più a trovar a quante cose è buona la saliva o la paglia, ma a quanti mestieri è adoperato M., ed in quanti è riuscito mirabile. Scalco, mastro di casa, secretario, lettore, soprastante di frati, compagno di studio, poeta, medico e presidente del Concilio. Or vada via la S. V., e riformi una volta questa povera Chiesa difformata, e per me baci la mano a quei Reverendiss. ed Illustriss. Sig. Legati, ed al Reverendiss. di Trento; nè si lasci mancar nè denari nè altro che abbia io, e stia sana. ...

S. il Legato.

1545.viii.15: Casa (Venice, as ambassador of the Pope) to Gualteruzzi (Rome, as secretary to Cardinal Farnese):[29]
Magn. M. Carlo.
La lettera vostra è degli 8 d'Agosto, del qual dì fu la mia. Dico che mi maraviglio che il Cardinal Farnese abbia chiesta la canzona, perchè Sua Signoria Reverendissima non dovea poter sapere che io l'avessi fatta; e Dio voglia che la non si divulghi e

---

[27] *Opere* (1806) 4:201.
[28] *Opere* (1806) 4:371.
[29] *Opere* (1806) 4:211.

siami di biasimo, come a poeta e come a legato, perchè la è mala poesia, e la poesia in se non conviene a quest'altr'arte: e senza fallo, se la va a torno, alcuni e molti diranno il vero, che io attendo alle baje. Bacio la mano a Mons. Reverendissimo Bembo del buono officio e favore, che Sua Signoria Reverendissima mi ha fatto. ...

Gio. vostro.

1545.ix.05: Casa (Venice, as ambassador of the Pope) to Gualteruzzi (Rome, as secretary of Cardinal Farnese):[30]
Magn. M. Carlo.
... Mi raccomando al Beccardello ovunque si sia, e al Cardinal nostro bacio la mano: ed or che le notti son più lunghe e più fresche, son risoluto pagar i miei debiti lealmente; benchè sieno moltiplicati sopra le mie forze, e benchè io legga lezioni, che finiranno, non avendo mai potuto trovare un pedante a'miei putti, che braman di volere studiare. Ho promesso ad Annibale un sonetto, come recita la Buccolica e l'Eunnunco a mente, senza errare più che dieci volte per ciascuna, e mi ha intimate per domani a otto: sì che converrà che io parli col cassiere, ed anche i Franciosi mi sollecitano; benchè di quelle cose fatte a caso ne ho piene le casse. State sano.

Gio. vostro.

1545.x.22: Casa (Venice, as ambassador of the Pope) to Gualteruzzi (Rome, as secretary of Cardinal Farnese):[31]
Magn. M. Carlo.
... Mi duole che io sento che il sonetto del ritratto è divulgato per Roma: ed io non l'ho mandato se non a voi, e poi l'ho mutato in mille luoghi che non istava ben prima, nè anche ora sta bene. Io son tanto debitore a quella Magnifica Madonna, che io mi vergogno a partirmi senza mostrarle almeno il buon voler mio. ...

Gio. vostro.

---

[30] *Opere* (1806) 4:209.
[31] *Opere* (1806) 4:210.

1545.xi.26: Casa (Venice, as ambassador of the Pope) to Gualteruzzi (Rome, as secretary of Cardinal Farnese):[32]
Magn. M. Carlo.
... Sono entrato in un laberinto di tradur certe cose greche in latino, e così mi convien far tregua con le muse e con Tiziano; benchè io sia sollecitato pur da'miei creditori, con li quali oramai ho bisogno di'intercessori, che io son troppo lungo spazio contumace. Baciate la mano a Mons. Reverendissimo Bembo, e state sano.

Gio. vostro.

1548.i.28: Casa (Venice, as ambassador of the Pope) to Gualteruzzi (Rome, as secretary of Cardinal Farnese):[33]
Signor M. Carlo osservandiss.
... La magnifica Quirina per quel che io posso comprendere, vorrebbe che i sonetti fossero lasciati nell'ordine che il Cardinal gli aveva posti; e certo, avendo Sua Signoria Reverendissima deliberato pensatamente quest'ordine, come io intendo, il mutarlo arà bisogno di scusa, e toccherà a voi a farla; e mi pare che voi me ne scriveste già non so che, ed io non guardai a ciò, non sapendo che il Cardinale avesse voluto più un ordine che un altro: però pensatevi sie meglio. E state sano.

Gio. vostro.

1548.ix.29: Casa (Venice, as ambassador of the Pope) to Gualteruzzi (Rome, as secretary of Cardinal Farnese):[34]
Signor M. Carlo osservandiss.
... Quanto alle stampe io mi rimetto a quello che il Quirini scriverà: dico alle stampe delle opere del Cardinal Bembo buona ed ottima mem., e quanto alle mie cose volgari io non credo però che V. S. mi consigliasse a stamparle, e meno in compagnia di quelle di Sua Signoria Reverendissima; però vi piacerà aspettare che elle sieno più e migliori, e così dico anche delle latine. Nostro Signor Dio vi conservi.

Gio. vostro.

---

[32] *Opere* (1806) 4:212.
[33] *Opere* (1806) 4:285.
[34] *Opere* (1806) 4:311–12.

1550.viii.09: Casa (Rome) to Beccadelli (Venice, as ambassador of the Pope):[35]
Reverendiss. Sig. e Padr. mio Osservandiss.
   ... Io ho venduto il mio Chericato a M. Cristoforo Cencio Romano 19m. scudi d'oro, e N. S. s'è contento ammettere la risegna; e così andrò seguitando di prepararmi per l'avvenire a vita più tranquilla secondo è stato sempre il mio desiderio. ...
Ser. Aff. L'Arciv. di Benevento

1551.ii.07: Casa (Rome) to Vettori (Florence):[36]
Molto Magn. Signore.
   Ho avuto il Dialogo stampato, ed ho veduto come V. Sig. persevera in giovare alla nostra Patria, insegnando a'suoi cittadini le buone lettere, e sollecitandogli con ogni industria a questi nobili studj, de'quali io non so se alcuna opera umana sia migliore. Per la qual sua industria io l'amo ognora più, come benefattore della mia Città; e certo il piacer ch'io sento che V. Sig. impieghi le sue forze in questo, m'ha fatto dire queste poche parole, essendo io naturalmente poco blando: e tanto più le dico volentieri e di cuore, poichè io ho veduto che Ella non s'è affaticata indarno, anzi ha fatto maggior numero di dotti scolari Ella sola, che forse non hanno fatto tutte le Città d'Italia, come io ho veduto per lo Spini e per il Ricasoli e per molti altri. Or ch'Ella desideri scrivermi più speso a me è gratissimo; e più grato mi è ch'Ella scriva latino, com'Ella dice, che altrimenti: ma Ella avrà in ciò male esercitarsi meco così debole e poco esercitato lottatore; nondimeno io la prego che non resti per questo, nè per le mie podagre, ch'io risponderò come quando mi sia lecito, e leggerò sempre volentieri anzi con mia dilettazione ed utilità le sue lettere. N. Sig. Dio la conservi.
Serv. L'Arcivesc. di Benevento

---

[35] *Opere* (1806) 4:376.
[36] *Opere* (1806) 2:199–200.

1551.iv.15: Casa (Rome) to Beccadelli (Venice, as ambassador of the Pope):[37]
Rever. Sig. e Padron mio Osserv.
... Del mio venire a Venezia sono pure in quella medesima inresoluzione ch'io le scrissi altre volte. ...
Ser. Affez. L'Arciv. di Benevento

1551.iv.25: Casa (Rome) to Beccadelli (Venice, as ambassador of the Pope):[38]
Reverendiss. Mons. mio Osservandiss.
... Io non posso scriver a V. S. Reverendiss. di mia mano, per esser da X. giorni in qua in letto con le podagre, le quali mi sono tuttavia più moleste: d'ogni cosa sia ringraziato il Signor Dio, il conservi V. S. in sua grazia. ...
S. Affezionatiss. L'Arciv. di Benevento

1552.iii.1: Casa (Venice) to Astorre Paleotti (Florence, in the house of Cardinal Farnese):[39]
Al magnifico signor messer mio osservandissimo. A Firenze appresso l'illustrissimo Cardinal Farnese

Ho commession da Nostro Signore molto espressamente di andar al concilio a questa prossima sessione. Io farò una honesta replica et poi perseverando Sua Beatitudine andrò ad obedir con mio molto incommodo dell'animo et del corpo et così abandonerò le ode et mal potrò servir monsignor illustrissimo nostro patrone della ode che Sua Signoria reverendisima desidera sopra la varietà della fortuna oltra che havendo parlato di questa materia sì nobil poeta come è Horatio oltra i Greci io sarei riputato temerario a intrarci; pur se io harò otio vedrò di dir a ogni modo qualche semplicità per contentar il cardinale. L'ode ch'io dico d'Horatio è nel primo libro Carmina 35, *O diva gratum, quae regis Antium.* I sonetti di quei signori sono excellentissimi et ben possono contentar Sua Signoria illustrissima sanza miei versi latini.

Se io havessi hauto tanto animo harei mandato la mia ode sopra l'adula‹zione› [burned] ch'io la mandassi poichè la è pur ve‹nu›ta alle mani di Sua Signoria Reverendissima et è ... [burned] per quel

---
[37] *Opere* (1806) 4:379.
[38] *Opere* (1806) 4:380.
[39] Santosuosso, "Inediti casiani," 493–94. Paleotti had been a friend since student days.

ch'io veggo scorre et ve ne mando una copia; et quanta alla comparatio della matrigna io ho voluto dir così: *Blanditiae norunt perdere mentem credulam non secus ac male novercae cum mendicant, olim mortiferas dapes multo melle*; la qual comparatione sarebbe intera e compita se havessi detto di più: *norunt perdere privignos*. Questa comparatione così come io la ho posta mi è stata lodata da i miei amici di Roma assai; et, quanto che ella sia lontana, non par loro così perchè, come la dolcezza delle parole ricopre il danno che ci fan gli adiectivi, così il mele delle vivande che porgono le matrigne ricopre il veleno che è in entro. Et quanto a questo forse ho dato noia a chi che sia, cioè che la comparatione non sia compita di esprimer con le parole, anco è parso a detti miei amici con i quali io soglio conferir queste mie bagattelle, che la sia espressa a bastanza, et che il finirla più oltre le togliesse più tosto vaghezza che no, massimamente seguitando incontenente quel verso: *Vivo imbuta malo dulcia murmura*, che par che replichi et dichiari la comparatione, dando quegli accidenti al susurro della adulatione, che le matrigne danno alle loro vivande, cioe' la dolcezza e 'l veleno. Et io credo che i poeti massime i lirici habbino rispetto a lasciar un poco di desiderio nella mente de lettori che alcuna volta anco aggiugne novità et dignità alle scritture. Per non ... dirò solo uno ‹esempio› ... di Horatio assai simile al mio s'io non ‹mi› sono ingannato. Nel primo libro Carmina 16 che comincia: *O matre pulchra*, nella quale leggerete: *Non Dindymene, non adytis quatit, mentem sacerdotum nuda Pythius Non Liber quoque, non acuta sic geminat Corybantes aera, Tristes ut irae*; dove per compir di explicar la comparatione era necessario dire et aggiugnere: *quatiunt mente nostras*, per cio' che Horatio vuol dir così che nè Cibele, nè Apollo scuote così la mente de suoi sacerdoti, nè Bacco nè i suoi ministri scuotono sì i lor instrumenti come la ira scuote non quei sacerdoti nè quegli instrumenti, ma gli animi nostri. Parse dunque a Horatio che la sua comparatione dovesse esser manco satievole mozza che la non sarebbe stata intera. ...

1552.iii.02: Casa (Venice) to Pier Vettori (Florence):[40]
Molto Magn. Sig. mio osservandiss.
   Fui impedito appunto in su l'ora dello scrivere Mercoledi

---

[40] *Opere* (1806) 4:156–58.

passato, sicchè io non potetti rispondere alle lettera di V. S., e poi ho avuto un'altra lettera con il quinterno delle sue annotazioni. [Vettori had sent verses communicating the desire of Giambattista Strozzi to acquire the country estate that Casa inherited from his father. With elaborate courtesy and compliments Casa declines before turning to the second letter.]

Ho veduto diligentemente le annotazioni di V. S., le quali mi pajono tutte vere e tutte nuove e chiare e latine, per la qual cosa io esorto V. S. a mandarle fuori oggimai; e la ringrazio che la mi ami tanto, che ella attribuisca troppo più al mio giudizio, che esso non vale.

Avendo io più ozio e un poco di più sanità, che io non soglio, mi era posto a rileggere i Poeti, massime i Greci, intermessi da me lungo tempo;[41] e leggendogli, mi è venuto fatto dei' versi latini, come V. S. ha veduto, benchè i miei versi non sono scritti a lei e a' suoi pari, se ella ha perciò alcun pari, *sed Consentinis, etc.* e per questa cagione io non ho mai avuto ardir di mandarglieli.

M. Paolo Manuccio mi ha mostro il proemio del suo libro delle antichità di Roma, per lo quale veggo, che esso scrive anche *de familiis*, e debbene scrivere assai bene e lungo, perchè di sei libri mostra che se ne consumi uno in questa cognizion sola. Io non so se il libro del nostro Padre Borghino sia in questa materia. M. Paolo è molto vicino a stampare i suoi. Dubito che io sarò costretto di andarmene al Concilio adesso, e così il mio ozio sarà durato poco. Bacio la mano di V. S. Nostro Signor Dio la conservi.

Di V. S. Serv. L'Arciv. di Benevento

1552.iii.09: Casa (Venice) to Vettori (Florence):[42]
Molto Magn. Signore.

Io scrissi Sabato, anzi Mercoledì passato, che M Paolo Manuccio stamperebbe il suo libro *de antiquitatibus*; ho poi riparlato con Suo Signoria, ed inteso che comincerà fra due o tre mesi, e che non ne stamperà se non quattro libri, e così il trattato *de familiis*, che era nel quinto libro, rimarrà indietro per ora. [Casa adds that there is still time for Vettori to send corrections to Caesar's *Commentaries*, then turns to academic gossip: Robortello

---

[41] Cf. Horace, *Carm.* IV.1.1, *intermissa, Venus, diu rursus bella moues*, and Introduction, part II.
[42] *Opere* (1806) 4:160.

has been called to the chair of Greek in Padua, as third choice. The second choice, Romulo, refused; and the first choice, Vettori, was never asked because Casa had spread the word that Vettori could not be lured to leave Florence.]

Ancorchè, come io scrissi Mercoledì, i miei versi sieno fatti *Tarentinis et Consentinis*; pur poichè vanno attorno, è meglio che io stesso li mandi a V. S., così le ho fatto far una copia di quel ch'io scrivo in memoria di Mons. Ubaldino. . . .

Serv. L'Arciv. di Benevento

1553.i.27: Casa (Venice) to Vettori (Florence):[43]

Io aveva prima molta obbligazione a Senofonte per tanti ammaestramenti che mi aveva dato, benchè poco osservati da me.
. . .

[Casa praises Vettori's emendations of Xenophon. He speaks of trip to Florence and hope of conversation with Vettori and Borghini, but was delayed at Rome until summer overtook him, which he wished to pass in Venice because of gout and to avoid soldiers in Bologna.[44] He still would like to come.]

Non posso dire a V. Sig. il piacer ch'io sento, che il Cardinal Farnese sia in sì buona opinione di V. Sig. e di tutta la Città, come Ella mi scrive, e come io sento generalmente da ognuno; e poichè al buon voler di S. Sig. Illustriss. si è aggiunto sì nobil Maestro, non si debbe dubitare che il frutto del suo studio non sia per esser grandissimo. Io non ho mai creduto a niuno che abbia avuto l'animo vero S. Sig. Reverendiss. più pieno di vera affezione e servitù volontaria di me; perciò quando verrà a proposito a V. Sig. mi farà grazia di baciargli le mani a mio nome: la quale potrebbe ancor un dì onoratamente cavare del Pistrino l'amico, che ha presso che finito l'opra; che se gli fia ricordato all'occasioni, lo farà.[45] Aspetto questa State con desiderio, perchè per veder l'opra di V. S. perchè l'ozio che m'è concesso dalle mie po-

---

[43] *Opere* (1806) 2:201–3.

[44] The trip mentioned must either be a brief return to Rome, otherwise undocumented, or the original departure from Rome, which in fact was delayed and overtaken by summer: in which case, at the beginning of 1553 Casa recalls events of the middle of 1551.

[45] Casa suggests that the favor he asks Vettori, of greeting the cardinal on his behalf, might one day free him, Casa, from "the Grind," i.e., the mill, as a place of toilsome bondage, punishment?, since he has nearly finished the "work": at the beginning of 1553 what can this mean? *Galateo*? Why does Casa need to be reminded to finish? Can there be a reference to a poem demanded by the cardinal?

dagre non ha più molte occupazioni; e io mi son volto a passare il tempo leggendo; la qual cosa io non fo più volentieri con altro Libro, che con quel di V. Sig. ...
> Servitore di V. Sig. L'Archivescovo di Benevento

1553.vii.15: Casa (Venice) to Vettori (Florence):[46]
[no salutation]
... Son entrato in una briga non necessaria, cioè di far versi Latini, e credeva di potermene liberare a mia posta, ma mi interviene alcontrario, non solo perchè io stesso non me n'astengo così facilmente; ma ancora, perchè io son ricerco alle volte di farne da persone, alle quali io non ardisco negare, come è il Cardinal Farnese, e qualche altro. Ma veggio poi, che il compiacer loro è mia vergogna in due modi: l'uno perchè l'esser Poeta non è forse in tutto comportabile al mio grado; e l'altro perchè l'esser cattivo Poeta non è comportabile a nessun grado. Io ho fatt'un Oda ad istanza del Cardinal Farnese in laude di Mad. Margerita Sorella di Rè di Francia, o più tosto detto che la bisognerebbe fare, come V. S. vedrà, che gliele mando. V. Sig. ha in gran parte la colpa, che io sia ricerco, perchè ella mi ha messo in reputazione appresso S. Sig. Illustriss. e con le parole, e con le scritture: sia contenta ancora d'aver la briga di vederla, e di leggerla due volte, ed avvertirmi liberamente in generale, ed in particolare, senza rispetto alcuno; perchè la mia natura è di mutare, e di rimutare, ed ancora di rifar voluntieri, come quello, che non ho fretta. Io non ho dato fuori quest'Ode, e non la darò, se non sento prima il parere di V. S. ma il Cardinale m'ha fatto sollecitare assai. Sono anche stato sforzato a scriverne un'altra in laude del Cardinal Tornone, la quale di maggior nervo che questa; ma i tempi non concedono, che io la mandi. ...
> *[no signature]*

1553.viii.12: Casa (Venice) to Vettori (Florence):[47]
Ho avuto la lettera di V. Sig. un poco tardi, perchè io era in villa. Io leggo sempre volentierissimo le sue lettere; ma questa con tante mie lodi ho io letta, quanto V. Sig. può pensare, con piena mia soddisfazione, essendo sicuro, che quello che le piace convi-

---

[46] *Opere* (1806) 2:175–76.
[47] *Opere* (1806) 2:200.

ene che piaccia a ognun che sa. Io andrò acconciando quei luoghi che essa mi ricorderà, per soddisfarmi, che per ora non ho altro negozio che mi diletti più, che trastullarmi con le lettere. Il Cardinal Sant'Angelo m'ha tolto quell'Oda, così com'ella è, ma non resterò perciò di acconciarla, se io potrò. Ringrazio il gentilissimo Barbadori, e m'offero a S. Sig. ...

Di V. Sig. Serv. L'Arcivesc. di Benevento

1553.ix.25: Casa (Di Villa in Trevisana) to Vettori (Florence):[48]
[no salutation]

Io ebbi il libro di V. Sig. ... La pistola al Cardinal Farnese è copiosa, e pura e prudente, come l'altre Scritture di V. Sig. e se io debbo dire interamente il mio senno, ancora, non some, più bella dell'altre sue Epistole, che sempre mi son parute bellissime. ...

[Asks Vettori's opinion on Lucretius, who invokes goddess, then says gods pay no heed.]

Io me ne sto assai riposatamente leggendo questi miei Poeti, che mi son riusciti di più lunga opera che io non pensai a principio.[49]

1554.ii.13: Casa (Narvesa) to Beccadelli (Venice, as ambassador of the Pope):[50]
Reverendiss. Mons. mio Osservandiss.

Sono stato impedito dai miei dolori alcuni giorni, perciò non ho potuto risponder prima alle lettere di V. S. Reverendiss. Rispondo ora ringraziandola della informazion che ella mi ha scritta, e della vita del Card. Contarini, la qual vita io vo tessendo, e come che io non voglia che ella vada fuori col mio nome, nondimeno mi affaticherò quant'io posso per ornarla quanto possono ornar una vita sì chiara le mie deboli forze. È vero che io era intorno ai poeti repetiti da me *longo intervallo:* ma io li ho posti giù finchè io finisca questa opera, alla quale mi sento poco atto in verità, ma V. S. e gli Eccellentissimi parenti saranno Signori sempre e di mostrarla e di nasconderla. Dovrò averla recata a fine in non lungo tempo, se il Signor Dio mi concederà sanità e ozio. ...

S. affezionatiss. L'Arciv. di Benevento

---

[48] *Opere* (1806) 2:211–13.
[49] Remarks the beginning of reading: see 1552.iii.02 above. Also speaks of reading as an "opera," which is the word used for literary products as well: could this be intended by "opra" in another letter?
[50] *Opere* (1806) 4:381–82.

1554.iii.31:Casa (Venice) to Vettori (Florence):[51]
Molto Magn. Sig. mio osservandiss.

Non mi par che il proemio di Lucrezio si possa scusar meglio, che come V. S. lo scusa; nè perciò mi par bene scusato, come non pare anche a lei. ... Circa al pensiero, che V. S. ha d'interpretar quel poco di Poetica, che mi par che ci avanzi d'Aristotile, mi par che ella faccia grave peccato a non comentarla, e far profitto ed utile agli studiosi senza dubitar di offendere altri: perchè con la prudenza sua potrà ben dire le sue opinioni senza mordere alcuno, ed anche con laudare ognuno. E veramente, se ella nol fa, noi ed ella medesima riceverà torto.

Mando una ode a V. S. fatta da me con molta affezione d'animo, così fosse ella fatta con molta arte e con molta sufficienza; se le parerà che io muti alcuna cosa, la prego ce me ne avvisi liberamente. Mando anche un Sonetto al Barbadori fatto mezzo in farnetico, avendo io le podagre con vigilia perpetua. Sua Signoria lo leggerà una volta, e poi ne farà come si fa de'sogni. ...

Serv. L'Arciv. di Benevento

1554.vii.16:Casa (Venice) to Vettori (Florence):[52]
[no salutation]

Io sono stato alcuni dì in villa, e poi tornato, ho avuto forestieri che m'hanno occupato ed impedito che io non ho risposto alle sue dolcissime lettere, pigliando sicurtà della sua bontà e cortesia; massimamente che io aveva risposto in parte per Mes. Camillo, ed in parte aveva commesso al mio Abate che rispondesse, e desse a V. Sig. una Oda che il Cardinal Farnese m'ha fatto fare. Ho letto molte volte la risposta di V. Sig. o per dir meglio la mia Pistola, nella quale io non avrei che rispondere, s'Ella parlasse d'altri che di me; o avrei tante cose da lodare, quante son parole o lettere in essa. Or le posso dir solo, che lo stile è bellissimo e candidissimo, e le sentenze sono elette e ben collocate e ben ornate. Ma certo V. Sig. mi fa vergognare, lodandomi tanto di soverchio; perciò io la prego che la moderi il corso dell'amore verso di me, dal quale Ella è stata trasportata troppo oltre ogni termine. So bene che chi mi vuol pur lodare convien che dica le bugie; ma io desidero ch'elle sieno almeno tollerabili.

---

[51] *Opere* (1806) 4:164.
[52] *Opere* (1806) 2:207–8.

Contuttociò io la ringraziio del suo infinito amore in verso di me, e me le raccomando di tutto cuore. N. Sig. Dio la consoli.

Serv. di V. Sig. L'Arcivesc. di Benevento

1554.ix.01: Casa (Venice) to Vettori (Florence):[53]
[no salutation]

... Se io avrò affaticato V. Sig. con tanto cattiva lettera, sia contenta di perdonarmi, e d'incolpar di ciò le podagre o chiragre, che par mi percuotino più voluntieri le dita che scrivono, che altra parte, volendomi forse ammonire, comechè tardi, che io lasci star l'arte ch'io non so fare. ...

Serv. L'Arciv. di Benevento

1554.xi.13: Casa (Trevisana? Venice? cf. "cinque mesi" below) to Denis Lambin (Lyon?).[54]
Ioannes Casa Cionysio Lambino s.d.

Accepi literas tuas humanissime scriptas, easdemque purissimas, atque elegantissimas. Carmen autem, & libentissime legi, & vehementer probavi: est enim, cum dignitate sententiarum grave, tum splendore verborum, & numerorum iucunditate illustre, atque concinnum. Sane intellego nihil fuisse, cur Calliope illa nostra inops, quam tu tamen dilaudas, tantum susciperet itineris, cum tu isthic adesses, qui Cardinalis Turnonii, hominis omni laude cumulati virtutem non modo exponere, id quod nos facere nostris versibus conati sumus, sed etiam abundanter ornare, & copiose augere facile posses. Suppudet itaque me; in sylvam enim ligna scilicet.

Sed tamen nihilominus Blanketo meo, homini conglutinandarum amicitiarum studiosissimo, magnam habeo gratiam; cujus opera factum esse intellego, ut ego te ista doctrina ornatum, ista scribendi facultate praeditum, non modo cognitum, sed etiam amicum habeam.

Ac doleo mehercule plurimum, cum vos Venetiis essetis, non frequentasse me vestram domum; quod ut facerem, coegerunt me Reipublicae tempora, & mea. Carui quidem certe uberibus fructibus, & magna iucunditate consuetudinis tuae. Cum enim tua haec ipsa scripta admirans, ab iis, quibus te bene cognitum certo scirem, per-

---

[53] *Opere* (1806) 2:178.
[54] *Opere* (1707) 3:274.

cunctatus diligentius essem de te, reperiebam id, quod mea ipse sponte animo iam antea statueram, atque perspexeram. Docuit enim me Nasius noster, itemque alii multi, de perpolita, elegantique doctrina, deque singulari probitate, atque humanitate tua.

Itaque sic tibi persuadeas velim, factum me tibi esse amicissimum, vel Musarum causa, quas ego a puero amavi plurimum, atque colui, quibusque gratissimum te esse intelligo; vel quod te Vir amplissimus, quem ego unum maxime omnium semper sum admiratus, amat, atque in honore habet; vel quod amantissimis literis, gravissimoque, ad dulcissimo carmine amorem erga te excitasti, atque inflammasti meum. Illud etiam mihi a te gratissimum accidit, quod Horatii Farnesii miserum casum, atque horribilem versibus praeclarissimis deplorans, egregium adolescentem, in quo Italia iamdudum iacentis spes nitebantur, divinis laudibus celebrasti.

Praeter quam enim quod omnis nostra natio hos lectissimos Farnesios fratres, maximo illorum merito, carissimos habet (nihil enim his praeclarissimis adolescentibus amabilius fieri, aut excogitari potest) mihi privatim quoque vetus cum clarissima illorum familia amicitia intercedit, multis illorum in me beneficiis, perpetuaque mea erga illos observantia confirmata. Quapropter sic habeto, me virtutem, doctrinam, humanitatem tuam, uti debeo, plurimi facere, semperque facturum esse, meamque voluntatem, meaque omnia tam tibi parata esse scito, quam quae sunt tua. Cardinali Turnonio viro maxime illustri, quem ego, & colo, & revereor plurimum, multam saltutem meo nomine dicas velim. Vale. Idib. Novemb. Venet. Anno M. D. LIIII.

1555.i.23: Casa (Trevisana) to Vettori (Florence):[55]
Molto Magn. Sig. mio.

... Vorrei esser stato alla lezione di Pindaro e d'Eschilo, e certo ne ho ben bisogno, che avendo io alle volte avuto nome di Poeta, comechè a torte, dovrei intenderli, e ricordarmene molto meglio che io non fo. Ma vorrei perciò che la lezione si fosse letta in questo ozio e tranquillità veneziana, alla quale V. S. è invitata e desiderata ed aspettata da me sommamente. ...

[Offers hospitality and financial aid, if the hard times find Vettori in need]

---

[55] *Opere* (1806) 4:166–68.

Con tutti questi romori di guerra io mi sono stato cinque mesi in questa solitudine, dove il maggiore disturbo che io abbia sono le campane, che non mi lasciano alle volte pensare. ...

Serv. L'Arciv. di Benevento

1555.iv.26: Casa (Di villa sul Trevisano) to Vettori (Rome):[56]
Molto Magn. Sig. mio.

È vero che io avea consciuto per più d'una lettera di V. S. che il suo desiderio era di liberarsi dalle miserie presenti della nostra infelicissima patria, e fuggire anche quelle che pare che le soprastiano; anzi quando s'intese qui che V. S. era ito a Roma, io dissi a molti che interpretavano questa sua gita altrimenti, ch'ella era pure partita per sua recreazione, e non per altro. ... Quando pure Sua Beatitudine, occupata in altro, non abbracciasse V. S., credo che il Cardinal Farnese la riceverebbe volentieri; e che essa arebbe cagion di tenersi assai onorato in casa di tali Principi; e perciò sarei di parere che la non se ne discostasse, e se io posso fare alcuno ufficio in questo, V. S. mi avvertisca, che io farò sempre volentieri ogni cosa per lei. Io sono costretto a starmi qui questa state per conto della mia sanità, o più tosto della mia infermità, e poi sono anche costretto di andare a Benevento, e farò anche un altro debito ufficio di baciare i piedi a Nostro Signore; e se a V. S. tornerà comodo di venir qua io la riceverì tanto volentieri, e più che persona che potesse venire. Sopra tutto la prego, che piu tosto che tornare a casa, durante questo travaglio, pigli ogni partito, e che si vaglia di me, che posso sovvenirla senza alcuno incomodo, come la può sapere. Prego Nostro Signor Dio che la consoli.

Serv. L'Arciv. di Benevento

1555.vii.20: Rucellai (Rome) to Vettori (Florence):[57]
Al molto magnifico signor mio osservandisimo messer Piero Vettori. A Fiorenza.

Molto magnifico signor mio osservandissimo. Io sono stato due giorni a Frascati con Cardinal Farnese dove si è ragionato assai sopra la persona vostra. Et però Sua Signoria Illustrissima mi ha mostro che gli dispiace assaissimo che non sia possuto

---

[56] *Opere* (1806) 4:168–69.
[57] Santosuosso, "Le opere italiane," 47: British Library Ms. Add. 10272, fol. 9r–v.

trovar fin qui luogo per Vostra Signoria la quale conosce persona da non lassarla così smarrire nella troppa quiete. Et perchè è stato romor infinito et noto a tutta la corte, perchè pareva che i ministri di Nostro Signore fussi tutti o la maggior parte proposti o dependenti da Farnese, per il che ne è anco stato rimosso qualcuno di quei ch'erano già fermi et stabiliti, però non è parso al Cardinale di poterne propor anche degli'altri. Ma se serrà occasione Vostra Signoria sia certa che non mancherà; et dove varranno le parole o i ricordi Monsignor nostro anch'in ciò non si perderà occasione, il qual Monsignore non ha hauto tempo di poter scriver due versi a Vostra Signoria non che di rispondergli; et la prega che lo habbi per scuso fin che possa supplire come desidera. . . .

Di Vostra Signoria servitore affettionatissimo
Annibale Rucellai

1559.i.29: Rucellai (Bologna) to Vettori (Florence):[58]
Al molto magnifico messer Piero Vettori mio signor osservandissimo. Firenze.

Molto magnifico signor mio osservandissimo. Quel che Monsignor della Casa bona memoria haveva intrapeso a scriver come opere da lassare per paragone del suo ingegno et della sua dottrina, rimasero alla sua morte monche et imperfette talmente che a mostrarle si vedrebbe sconciature et monstri, et non cose ben perfette et condutte al suo fine con la prudenza et giuditio che si conviene alle opere gravi; il che esso proprio conobbe morendo che ricordò si abbruciassero tutte le sue scritture di compositioni. Questo che si è dato fuora son tutte cose fatte da esso per puro esercitio. . . .[59] Andrem più adagio a dar fuora le cose latine et prima che se ne pigli resolutione le farò vedere a Vostra Signoria per intenderne 'l parer suo, poi ch'ella si contenta di pigliar questa fatica. Ringratiola con ogni affetto della pia affettione che veggo ch'ella porta a quella felice memoria, et le resto obligato con tutto 'l core della humanità che le è piaciuto di usare verso di me, che non ho risposto prima alla sua delli sette perch'ella è stata a Venetia donde me l'hanno rimandata in

---

[58] "Le opere italiane," 48–49: British Library Ms. Add. 10272, fols. 12v–13r.
[59] Rucellai refers to the first edition of *Galateo* by Erasmo Gemini, 1558, which Vettori had criticized for a remark against Dante.

qua, dove mi trovo pronto et desiderosissimo di servirla et obedirla come sarò sempre in ogni luogo. ...

Di Vostra Signoria, servitore
Annibale Rucellai

1559.xii.02: Rucellai (Rome) to Vettori (Florence):[60]
Al molto magnifico messer Piero Vittori mio signore osservandissimo. Firenze.

Molto magnifico signor mio osservandissimo. Ho da ringratiar assai Vostra Signoria della amorevolezza et diligenza, che le è piaciuto di usare con quei Giunta, acciochè quelle cose latine non sieno malmenate; et l'offerta ch'ella fa così efficace d'impiegar l'opera et iuditio suo intorno a ciò mi rende certo che Vostra Signoria persevera da vero et perfetto amico di quella felice memoria come ella fu sempre. Io mi lassai indirre a preghi di diversi parenti et amici ad acconsentire che si desse fuora quelle poche cose vulgari, che fu errore. Hora saprò di non poter fallire con il consiglio di Vostra Signoria alla quale mi parrà di potermene rapportare sicuramente essendo certo che dalla molta prudenza et virtù sue non si potrà pigliar se non ottima resolutione; però piglierò sicurtà dell'offerta che ella mi fa, per lassar esequir poi tutto ciò che a lei piacerà. Et come prima potrò, manderò tutto quel che ci è, che non sono però molte cose nè di momento. Non posso mandarle hora, havendole a Venetia con diverse altre scritture et robe, le quali non ho modo di far venir se non quando sia fatto il Papa. So che Monsignor della Casa non stimava nè honorava alcuno più di Vostra Signoria, così et molto più devo far io che le bacio la mano humilmente offerendomeli con tutto 'l core che Nostro Signor Dio la conservi felicemente. ...

Di Vostra Signoria servitore affezionatissimo
Annibale Rucellai

1560.v.07: Rucellai (Venice) to Vettori (Florence):[61]
Al molto magnifico messer Piero Vittori mio signore osservandissimo. Firenze.

Molto magnifico signor mio osservandissimo. Quand'a Dio piacque io finalmente mi condussi qua, et ho lassato a messer

---

[60] Santosuosso, "Le opere italiane," 49–50: British Library Ms. Add. 10272, fol. 14v.
[61] "Le opere italiane," 50: British Library Ms. Add. 10272, fol. 17r.

Stephan Carolo le cose latine di Monsignor della Casa bona memoria acciò che le faccia copiare in buona forma essendo la maggior parte in confusione et mal leggibile. Poi gli ho ordinato che mandi a Vostra Signoria tutto quel ch'è, che sarà poco; et ella piglierà fatica et resolutione di quanto le paia da esequire, poi che così si è degnata di voler fare per sua gratia et per l'amor et affettione che ella porta a quelle benedette ossa. Et sia certa Vostra Signoria ch'io ricevo questa sua opera per una delle maggior gratie ch'io potessi ricevere in questo mondo di che le resterò con perpetuo obligo; et le bacio la mano humilmente offerendomeli con tutto 'l core. ...

Di Vostra Signoria servitore affezionatissimo
Annibale Rucellai

1561.ix.06: Rucellai (Venice) to Vettori (Florence):[62]

Al molto magnifico signor Pietro Vettorii [mio sig]nore osservandissimo. Firenze.

Molto magnifico signor mio osservandissimo. La sua de 23 del passato mi è stata di somma consolatione per il pieno ragguaglio che mi dà sopra le cose di Monsignor bona memoria.

Io non havevo scrittone prima a Vostra Signoria per non affrettarla, pensando ch'ella havesse da considerar troppe cose da farlo in così breve tempo. Hor ch'ella mi dice haver visto et pensato a tutto maturamente, et che si satisfa assai, et giudica che quelle cose, tal qual'elle sono, sieno da dar fuora, mi par d'esser certo non poter errare co 'l consiglio del rivederle. Io non le mandai a Vostra Signoria con altro fine che di rapportarmi a quanto fosse il parer suo. Adesso che le piace, per sua bontà et per l'amore che porta a quella honorata memoria et a me, di pigliarsi anche questa altra pena del far usar diligenza ch'elle sieno riviste et stampate bene et correttamente, non voglio recusarla et accetto la sua amorevolissima oferta con quella prontezza che mi sforzerò anco di usare in ogni occasione per servitio suo, quando le occorresse valersi dell'opera mia.

Crederei che fosse a proposito nell'epistola dedicatoria che si farà, dar un poco di conto che tutte quelle son cose fatte dall'autore per suo esercitio semplicemente, perchè con effetto non vi è fatto opera nessuna, nè cosa de la quale Monsignor facessi gran

---

[62] "Le opere italiane," 51–53: British Library Ms. Add. 10272, fols. 18v–21r.

conto; [here Rucellai elaborates on his story of Casa's wish that the works be burned] ... le cose fatte da lui erano solo per puro esercitio, et per impatronirsi et farsi familiari hor i poeti et hor gl'oratori et altri autori secondo che scriveva in verso o in prosa. [Rucellai also promises to think to whom the works should be dedicated.]

Di Vostra Signoria servitore affezionatissimo
Annibale Rucellai

... Andrò cercando di epistole delle quali so che ne fece Monsignor nostro diverse, ma non ne teneva poi conto. ... [One sentence in a copious postscript devoted to other matters makes it appear that Vettori had requested letters to be included in the edition. Rucellai did not carry out his promise to search; late and rather rudely he explained why: 1564.iii.24 below]

1562.vi.20: Rucellai (Rome) to Vettori (Florence):[63]

Al molto magnifico messer Piero Vittori [mio signo]re osservandissimo. Firenze.

Molto magnifico signor mio osservandissimo. Non ho voluto sollecitare Vostra Signoria dopo che le scrissi l'anno passato di rapportarmi a lei quanto al stampar le cose latine di Monsignor nostro bona memoria, presumendomi che le fusse a quore questa cosa, come sua propria, secondo che mi certificate per la vostra delli 13 del presente. ...

[Rucellai mentions Cardinal De Tournon as someone to whom the book might have been dedicated, only that he is dead, so there is no one, he asserts, more deserving than Vettori himself. Rucellai also asks that the dedication to be printed under his name actually be composed by Vettori, to whom he also leaves the practical burdens of printing.]

Ne la epistola dedicatoria desidereri molto che Vostra Signoria fussi contenta per amor mio di affaticarsi assai in mostrar che nessuna cosa fu fatta mai dall'autore per opera, ma solo per esercitio; et che tutte queste cose sono fragmenti ecc., in che desidereri di quei concetti che sapete usar voi, i quali gusto quando li veggo et intendo io che no so già esprimerli hora. Però in

---

[63] "Le opere italiane," 53–54: British Library Ms. Add. 10272, fols. 22r–v.

somma mi rapporto totalmente a voi sapendo di non poter errare con la prudenza vostra. ...
> Di Vostra Signoria servitore et da figliolo obedientissimo
> Annibale Rucellai

1564.iii.21: Rucellai (Rome) to Vettori (Firenze):[64]

Al molto magnifico messer Piero Vettori mio signore osservandissimo. Firenze.

Molto magnifico signor mio osservandissimo. Conosco che nella epistola fatta da voi in mio nome è stato durato fatica de quore, et che ci havete impiegato drento la dottrina et l'ingegno mirabilmente.

[All the same, Rucellai suggests shortening and wonders if the "modern instance" of Guicciardini, cited as one would an ancient, will be accepted outside Tuscany.]

Queste cose non si hanno da intitolare ad altri che a voi, però, se vi paresse da inserirlo in questa epistola, fate voi, ricordandovi ch'ella ha da apparir scritta da me a voi, et che mi si conviene far qualche mentione delle virtù et dottrine vostre singulari, et de la reverenza che vi portava l'auttore, che mi han mosso etc. Ho visto la forma de la lettera et del libro che mi pare riesca benissimo. ...
> Di Vostra Signoria servitore affezionatissimo
> Annibale Rucellai

1564.iii.25: Rucellai (Rome) to Vettori (Florence):[65]

Al molto magnifico messer Piero Vettori mio signore osservandissimo. Firenze.

Molto magnifico signor mio osservandissimo. ... Le scritture di monsignor bona memoria sono a Venetia, però non posso cercar epistole. Ricordomi che ve ne son certe, ben poche et che mal si potrien dar fuora; altre che ha scritte come a Vostra Signoria et a diversi, non so che se ne sia tenuto registro, et le minute debbono essersi smarrite, perchè io non ne ho notitia. Potrebbon esser fra certe cassacie di scritture qua ma bisognerà tempo a cercarle: però non posso mandarne a Vostra Signora

---

[64] "Le opere italiane," 61–62: British Library Ms. Add. 10272, fol. 40r–v.
[65] "Le opere italiane," 62: British Library Ms. Add. 10272, fol. 42r.

qualche numero come vorrei. Baciole la mano pregando Nostro Signore Dio che la conservi et feliciti. ...

Di Vostra Signoria servitore
Annibale Rucellai

1564.vi.10: Vettori (Florence) to Cardinal Farnese (Rome):[66]

All'illustrissimo et Reverendissimo Monsignore il signor Cardinal Farnese, signore et patron suo osservandissimo.

Illustrissimo et Reverendissimo mio Monsignore, Questa noia che io ho sopportato in rivedere queste fatiche di Monsignore della Casa, mi è stata di manco fastidio assai per havere io insieme sodisfatto all'obligo inverso l'amico et servito, con quanto amore io ho potuto all'honore di quella virtuosa memoria. V'ho di più sentito un non minor piacere, perchè ho trovate tutte queste sue opere piene di molta lode et gloria della vostra ilustrissima casa; e questo è intervenuto quasi dalla prima a l'ultima, et similmente verso ogni persona nata in quella, che tutte sono state celebrate meritatamente da esso, tal che questo diletto m'ha condotto infino al fine che mai m'ha lasciato. Hor poi che ne sono venuto a capo, m'è parso subito di mandarne un volumetto a Vostra Signoria illustrissima et Reverendissima acciò che ella veggha questi eterni testimonij (s'io non m'inganno) de suoi honori, benchè alla molta dignità et virtù di quella non troppo necessarii, de i quali pero io mi stimo che una parte non gli saranno nuovi, ma le sia bene nuovo che sieno messi insieme et fatti communi al mondo. Perchè (come ella vedrà) io ho posto diligenza in questo dargli fuora et aiutato questa impresa, quant'io ho potuto, m'è parso di potere mandarla come cosa, dove io habbia un poco di parte, a quella persona, alla quale io ho mandate con più ragione le cose mie proprie, se bene non di tanto valore et stima quanto son queste, nè tanto atte a spargere per tutto et perpetuare la sua fama. Vostra Signoria Reverendissima si degni di accettare questo picciol dono, et si conservi sana, comandandomi, quando io mi giudica atto ad alcuno suo servitio, come a suo huomo et fedel servitore, che le sarò sempre.

Di Vostra Signoria illustrissima et Reverendissima humil servitore
Pietro Vettori

---

[66] "Le opere italiane," 62–63: Biblioteca Comunale, Forlì: *Autografi Piancastelli* (Vettori).

BIBLIOGRAPHY

Alberigi, Giuseppe. *I Vescovi Italiani al Concilio di Trento (1545–1547)*. Florence, 1959.

Anderson, William S. "The Theory and Practice of Poetic Arrangement from Vergil to Ovid." In Fraistat: 44–65.

Balducci, G. *Il Palazzo Farnese in Caprarola illustrato nella storia e nell'arte*. Rome, 1910.

Barolini, Teodolinda. "The Making of a Lyric Sequence: Time and Narrative in Petrarch's *Rerum vulgarium fragmenta*." *Modern Language Notes* 104 (1989): 1–38.

Battistella, O. *Di Giovanni della Casa e altri letterati all'abbazia dei conti di Collalto in Nervesa intorno alla metà del secolo XVI*. Treviso, 1904.

Biadego, G. "Galeazzo Florimonti e il *Galateo* di Monsignor della Casa." *Atti del Reale Istituto Veneto* 60.2 (1900–1901): 530–57.

Campana, Lorenzo. "Monsignor Giovanni della Casa e i suoi tempi." *Studi storici* (Pisa), XVI (1907): 3–84, 247–69, 349–580; XVII (1908): 145–282, 381–606; XVIII (1909): 325–513.

Casa, Giovanni della. *Rime, et prose di M. Giovanni della Casa*. Venice: Nicolò Bevilacqua, 1558.

———. *Ioannis Casae Latina Monimenta*. Ed. Petrus Victorius. Florence: Giunta, 1564.

———. *Ioannis Casae Latina Monimenta*. Ed. Petrus Victorius. Florence: Giunta, 1567.

———. *Ioan. Casae Carmina et Orationes Plœrœque Thucydidis in Latinum Sermonem Ab Eodem Conversae. Ex illius monumentis, anno abhinc ferè quinquagesimo primum editis a Petro Victorio v. c. l.* Ed. Iohannes Caselius. Helmstadt: In Acad. Iulia Excudebat Iacobvs Lvcivs, 1610.

———. *Opere*. Ed. G. B. Casotti. Florence: G. Mannin, 1707.

———. *Ioannnis Casae Latina Monimenta*. Ed. Nicolaus Hieronymus Gundlingius. Magdeburg: Officina Libraria Rengeriana, 1709.

———. *Opere*. Ed. G. Verdani. Venice: A. Pasinelli, 1728.

———. *Opere di Monsignor Giovanni della Casa Dopo l'edizione di Fio-*

renza del MDCCVII. e di Venezia del MDCCXXVIII. molto illustrate e di cose inedite accresciute. Naples, 1733. 6 vols.
——. *Opere* ("Accresciuta e Riordinata"). Ed. G. Verdani. Venice: A. Pasinelli, 1752.
——. *Opere di Monsignor Giovanni della Casa.* Milan: Società Tipografica de'Classici Italiani, 1806. 4 vols.
——. *Galateo.* Ed. Gennaro Barbarisi. Venice: Marsilio, 1991.
——. *Se si debba prendere moglie. Galateo.* Ed. Arnaldo Di Benedetto. I classici italiani TEA. Turin: UTET, 1992.
Coffin, David R. *The Villa in the Life of Renaissance Rome.* Princeton: Princeton University Press, 1979.
Cosenza, Mario Emilio. *Biographcal and Bibliographical Dictionary of the Italian Humanists and of the World of Classical Scholarship in Italy, 1300–1800.* Boston: G. K. Hall, 1962.
Costa, G. *La leggenda dei secoli d'oro nella letteratura italiana.* Bari: Laterza, 1972.
Cremante, R. in V. Branca, ed., *Dizionario Critico della Letteratura Italiana.* Turin, 1973. I: 688–92.
D'Amico, John. *Renaissance Humanism in Papal Rome.* Baltimore: Johns Hopkins University Press, 1983.
Douglas, Mary. *Rules and Meanings: The Anthropology of Everyday Knowledge.* Harmondsworth, 1973.
Durling, Robert M., ed. and trans. *Petrarch's Lyric Poems. The* Rime Sparse *and Other Lyrics.* Cambridge, Mass.: Harvard University Press, 1976.
Endres, Clifford. *Joannes Secundus: The Latin Love Elegy in the Renaissance.* Hamden, 1981.
[Flacius, Matthias]. *Epistola de more Pauli Tertij Pont. Max. deque iis quae ei post mortem eius acciderunt.* Piacenza [sc. Basel], 1549.
Fraenkel, Eduard. *Horace.* Oxford, 1957.
Fraistat, Neil. *Poems in Their Place: The Intertextuality and Order of Poetic Collections.* Chapel Hill: University of North Carolina Press, 1986.
François, Michel. *Le Cardinal François de Tournon: Homme D'Ètat, Diplomate, Mécène, et Humaniste (1489–1562).* Paris: E. de Boccard, 1951.
Gaj, F. and E. Guj. *Palazzo Farnese in Caprarola.* Rome, 1895.
Goffman, E. *Interaction Ritual: Essays on Face-to-Face Behavior.* New York, 1967.
Goudet, J. "La fécondité du verbe et la poésie de Della Casa." *Revue des études italiennes* 17 (1971): 293–317; 18 (1972): 30–60.
Grafton, Anthony. *Joseph Scaliger: A Study in the History of Classical Scholarship.* Oxford, 1983. Vol. I.

———, and Lisa Jardine. *From Humanism to the Humanities*. Cambridge, Mass.: Harvard University Press, 1986.

———, with April Shelford and Nancy Siraisi. *New Worlds, Ancient Texts: The Power of Tradition and the Shock of Discovery*. Cambridge, Mass.: Harvard University Press, 1992 (1995).

Kristeller, Paul Oskar. "The Editing of Fifteenth-Century Texts: Tasks and Problems." *Italian Culture* 4 (1983): 115–22.

———. *Iter Italicum*. London: Warburg Institute; Leiden: Brill, 1992. VI: 353b–354b. Codices Vaticani Latini 14825–14837.

Ley, Klaus. *Die "scienza civile" des Giovanni della Casa. Litteratur als Gesellschaftskunst in der Gegenreformation*. Heidelberg, 1984.

Longhi, Silvia. "Il tutto e le parti nel sistema di un canzoniere (Giovanni della Casa)." *Strumenti Critici* 39–40 (1979): 265–300.

Maddison, C. *Marc Antonio Flaminio: Poet, Humanist, Reformer*. London, 1965.

McCarren, V. P. *A Critical Concordance to Catullus*. Leiden, 1977.

Nichols, Fred J., ed. and trans. *An Anthology of Neo-Latin Poetry*. New Haven: Yale University Press, 1979.

Perosa, A. and J. Sparrow, eds. *Renaissance Latin Verse: An Anthology*. London: Duckworth, 1979.

Piazzoni, A. M. and P. Vian. *Manoscritti Vaticani Latini 14666–15203, Catalogo Sommario*. Città del Vaticano: Biblioteca Apostolica Vaticana, 1989.

Prosperi, A. *Tra Evangelismo e Controriforma: G. M. Giberti (1495–1543)*. Rome, 1969.

Puelma, Mario. "Die Aitien des Kallimachos als Vorbild der römischen Amores-Elegie." *Museum Helveticum* 39 (1982): 1–46, 287–304.

Putnam. *See* Van Sickle, 1980.

Race, W. H. *The Classical Priamel from Homer to Boethius*. Mnemosyne Supplement 74. Leiden, 1982.

Rebhorn, Wayne. "Della Casa, Giovanni." In *Dictionary of Italian Literature*. Coed. Peter and Julia C. Bondanella. Westport, Conn.: Greenwood Press, 1979: 166.

Saccone, Eduardo. *Le buone e le cattive maniere: Letterature e Galateo nel cinquecento*. Bologna: Il Mulino, 1992.

Santirocco, Matthew. *Unity and Design in Horace's Odes*. Chapel Hill: University of North Carolina Press, 1986.

Santosuosso, Antonio. "Inediti casiani con appunti sulla vita, il pensiero, e le opere dello scrittore fiorentino." *La rassegna della letterature italiana* 79 (1975): 461–95.

———. "Books, Readers and Critics: The Case of Giovanni della Casa, 1537–1975. The First Editions." *La Bibliofilia* 79 (1977): 130–180.

———. "Le opere italiane del Casa e l'edizione principe di quelle latine nei carteggi vettoriani del British Museum." *La Bibliofilia* 79 (1977): 37–68.

———. *The Bibliography of Giovanni della Casa: Books, Readers, and Critics, 1537–1975.* Florence: Olschki, 1979.

———. *Vita di Giovanni Della Casa.* Rome: Bulzoni, 1979.

Scarpati, Claudio. *Studi sul Cinquecento italiano.* Milan: Università Cattolica del Sacro Cuore, 1982.

Sole, Antonio, *Cognizione del Reale e Letteratura in Giovanni Della Casa.* Rome: Bulzoni, 1981.

Tarrant, R. J. "*Da Capo* Structures in Some *Odes* of Horace." In *Homage to Horace: A Bimillenary Celebration.* Ed. S. J. Harrison. Oxford: Clarendon Press, 1995. 3–49.

Tateo, F. "Il mondo arcadico e i temi della cultura umanistica." In *Tradizione e realtà nel umanesimo italiano.* Bari: Laterza, 1967. 41ff.

Ubaldinus, Johannes Paulus, ed. *Carmina poetarum nobilium studio conquisita.* Milan: Antonius Antonianus, 1563.

Van Sickle, John. "Propertius (*uates*): Augustan Ideology, Topography, and Poetics in Eleg. IV,1." *Dialoghi di Archeologia* 8 (1975): 116–45.

———. "Bucoliche 11: La Struttura." *Enciclopedia Virgiliana.* Rome, 1984. I: 549–52.

———. *Poesia e Potere: Il Mito Virgilio.* Rome-Bari, 1986.

———, ed. *Augustan Poetry Books*, issue of *Arethusa* 13 (1980): including Putnam, M. C. J. "Propertius' Third Book: Patterns of Cohesion": 97–113; Van Sickle, John. "The Bookroll and Some Conventions of the Poetic Book": 5–42; and Zetzel, J. E. G. "Horace's *Liber Sermonum*: The Structure of Ambiguity": 59–77.

Zetzel. *See* Van Sickle, 1980.

INDEX

Aesop: 10
Alcaeus, ode sought in tradition of: 26, 34
allusion, cf. emulation
   7, 8, 9, 10, 18, 19
Aristotle, *Ethics*: 11, 12, 123, 124, 125
   ethical-aesthetic middle way: 27

Bandinelli, Ubaldino (d. 1551): 21, 87, 134
Beccadelli, Lodovico (1501–1571?): 6–7, 15, 20, 120–22, 126, 127, 130, 131
Bembo, Pietro Cardinal (1470–1547): 1, 5–6, 9, 11, 13, 124, 126, 128
   cardinalate: 15
   idealized portrait by Casa: 85–86
   posthumuous poetry-book (q.v.): 16, 114, 129
Berni, Francesco (1497?–1535): 7, 88
Boccaccio, Giovanni (1313–1375)
   emulated by Casa: 3
   fate of Italian and Latin works differs: 4
   gynaikophobia shared by Casa: 88

Callimachus
   aesthetics in Casa: 104
   in poetics of Propertius (q.v.): 79–80

Camena, cf. Muses: 87
   Greek and Italic combined: 105
canzoniere (song-book, cf. poetry-book)
   posthumous of Bembo (q.v.): 114
Casa, Giovanni della (1503–1556)
   ambivalent relations to model of Petrarch (q.v.): 1, 2, 6, 84
   appointments by Pope Julius III refused:
     to Council of Trent: 19, 131
     to France as nuncio: 16
   cardinalate sought vainly: 2, 3
   fates of work in Italian and Latin (q.v.):
     fame of *Galateo* and *Rime*: 3–4, 120
     gradual oblivion of *Monumenta*: 4–5
   friend of Bembo (q.v.): 1, 5, 9, 13–16, 18, 85, 126–29
   ideology, sc. pride, cf. *Latium*
     in Florence: 93, 95, 109
     in Greek and Latin: 93–94
     in Italy and Farnese (q.v.) power, cf. Hesperia: 81, 101, 106, 139
   poetics, sc. metapoetry, cf. Muses
     Catullan, Horatian vocabulary assimilated: 103
     claimed pastoral (q.v.) origins: 105

middle way: 27, 81, 102
  thin (*ben magro*): 123
  poetry as journey: 26
    as enslavement: 21, 134
    as financial transaction: 109
  sexuality problematic: 6, 7-8, 12-13, 120-21, 124-25
  will to burn works: 1, 141
Castalia (place of Muses, q.v.): 94, 99
Catullus
  candida (white) for mistress echoed: 96
  Carm.
    1.1 *libellum*: 103, 113
    16.1, 16 ring structure (q.v.): 104
    25.12 *minuta magno* (tiny grand): 103
    34.5-6 *progenies* (child): 98
    36.1, 20 ring structure (q.v.): 104
    49.6-7 *optimus* (best): 104
    50.4 *uersiculos* (verselets): 103
    95.10 *populus* (people): 104
  in Casa's poetics: 30, 103
  nugae (poetic trifles): 97
  style appropriated
    sensuous details: 36, 96
    word arrangement of *Carm*. 65.5-6: 113
Cicero
  read in country by Casa while Rome burned: 6
  rural retreat to write: 2, 5
classical Greek and Roman authors
  cf. Aesop, Alcaeus, Aristotle, Catullus, Cicero, Euripides, Hesiod, Horace, Propertius, Tibullus, Virgil
Contarini, Gasparo Cardinal (1483-1542): 23, 136

Council of Trent: vii
  Casa's demurral: 19, 131
  "reform this deformed church": 127
country, cf. pastoral
  escape from corrupt city: 6
  exile from desired city: 109
  morally superior to city: 2, 27, 80, 82
  origin of poetry: 109

de Tournon, François Cardinal (1489-1562): 22, 31, 100, 138-39

emulation, cf. allusion
  by Casa
    of Bembo: 18
    of Horace: 30, 80, 99
  humanists of classics: 5
Euripides
  Hippolytus 616-50: 89
  Orestes 94-129: 83
  polemic against women, cf. Boccaccio: 18

Faerno, Gabriele (d. 1562): 84, 91
Farnese clan
  their patronage (*amicitia*) Casa's boast: 1, 139
  Alessandro (1468-1549), Cardinal (1493), Pope Paul III (1534): 1
    copyright to editor, benediction to readers of book by Bembo (q.v.): 114
    reads classical poets in country with grandson Alessandro: 6
    remembered at death of grandson Orazio: 108
  Alessandro Cardinal (a son of Pier Luigi: 1520-1589)

cardinalate precocious: 1
compared to Alexander the Great: 114
garden on Palatine Hill: 87
Gualteruzzi (q.v.) his secretary: 13
honored in posthumous book of Bembo (q.v.): 114, 115
inquires of poetry by Casa: 14, 126, 127
quarrel with Pope Julius III: 16
  commands *CL* VIII: 19, 97, 131
  commands *CL* XI: 21, 23, 106, 135, 137
  retreat to Florence, sees *CL* VII: 19, 91
relations with Pier Vettori (q.v.)
  flattered by: 4, 23, 33, 146
  guided in study by: 21
  his good will to assured by Casa: 140
  yet procures no office for: 24–25, 140–41
restored to influence by Pope Paul IV: 24, 140–41
villa at Caprarola: 10
Orazio (a son of Pier Luigi: 1522?–1554): 25–26, 106–7, 138–39
Ottavio (a son of Pier Luigi: 1521–1586): 14
Pier Luigi (a son of Alessandro: 1503–1547)
  raped Geri (q.v.): 13
  violent death: 16
Ranuccio (a son of Pier Luigi: Cardinal Sant'Angelo, 1530–1565): 22, 136
Flaminio, Marcantonio (1498–1550): 9, 14–15, 17, 80

Florimonte, Galeazzo (ca 1478–1567): 12, 17, 27, 81

Geri, Cosimo (1512–1537): 7–8, 121–24
  rape of: 13, 115
Giberti, Gian Matteo (1495–1543): 17
Gualteruzzi, Carlo (fl. 1540–post 1558): 3–5, 13, 29, 126–29
  editor posthumously
    of Bembo (q.v.) 15–16, 114, 129
    of Casa's Italian works: 3, 33

Hesiod, *Theogony* 1–103: 105
Horace
  allusive use of his language: 7, 20
  Ars Poetica 141 *captae* ... *Troiae* (Troy captured): 83
  as model emulated
    epistles: 9–10
    ethical-aesthetic ideal of middle way: 27, 81
    imagination rooted in country (q.v.): 2
    pastoral (q.v.) boyhood: 100
    poetics, vatic: 103
    vocabulary of: 103
    poetry-book (q.v.): 29–30, 99
    style of simile: 94
  Carm. (Odes), parade, I.1–11: 110
    I.1.3–4 *sunt quos curriculo* (Some with chariot): 98, 102
    I.16.1 *o matre pulchra* (o than fair mother): 96, 132
    I.24.1–4 *quis desiderio* (what for desire): 92
    I.34 *Fortuna*: 97
    I.35 *O diua* (o goddess): 97, 131
  Epist. 1.4.8–9 *quid uoveat* ... (what would vow): 7, 121

Epodes
    exile from city (2): 89–90
    gynaikophobic (8 and 17): 88
    vatic vein (1, 7, 14, 16): 90
read in country by Farnesi: 6
Roman Odes: 29–30, 80, 104, 106, 110
    III.3.69–72 *Quo, Musa* (Whither, Muse): 101
    III.4.1–20 *lucos, aquae, aurae* (groves, waters, breezes): 105
    III.4.2, 21 *Calliope, Camenae*: 105
    III.4.9–12 *puerum* (as a boy): 100
    III.4.21–22 *tollor* (I am lofted): 99
Serm.
    II.3.191 *capta ... Troia* (Troy captured): 83

Italy; cf. Casa, ideology

Lambin, Denis (1516–1572): 25, 138–39
Latin, cf. *Latium*
  letters in praised: 119
  mark of aristocratic culture: 4, 9, 27, 30–31
Latium cf. Latin
  association with Farnese (q.v.) power: 90, 98, 108
  echoing Virgil (q.v.): 95
  Golden Age returns to: 99
  invested with Virgilian melancholy: 107

Manuzio, Paolo (1512–1574): 133
metaphor
  love as wound: 83
  scholar as husbandman: 109, 110

writing poetry as journey: 26, 99
  as enslavement: 21, 134–35
  as exile: 110–11
  as financial transaction: 109
  as harvest: 111
meter: 28–31
  Alcaic dyad: 29, 104, 106
  Asclepiadean cycle: 29, 99
    fifth: 29, 109–10
    first: 20, 97
    second: 92, 98, 99
    third: 95
  dactylic: 28–29
    elegiacs: 79–81
    epigrams: 112–13
    hexameters: 83, 85
  Phalaecean: 29–30, 102
Molza, Francisco Maria (1489–1544): 6, 87
Muses, cf. *Camena*, Castalia
  Calliope: 110
  figurative for poetry: 11, 14, 86
  Melpomene: 94, 101
    in Horace & Casa: 99
  Pierian: 96
  Polyhymnia: 108
  Thalia: 103, 105, 107
  Thespian: 108
mythemes
  Chiron, Achilles' teacher: 110
  Cocytus: 81
  Cypris: 89
  Elysian fields: 81
  Giants assail heaven: 111
  Golden Age returns: 91, 99
  Helen and Troy: 83
  Hesperia, cf. Casa, ideology; Virgil: 91, 100, 107
  Justice flees Iron Age: 91
  Medea: 105

poetic origins: 94
   pastoral (q.v.) childhood: 105
   Siren song: 8, 121

pastoral
   ecclesiastical, cf. Florimonte, Giberti: 2, 17, 24
   literary, cf. Petrarch, Virgil
      allegory: 18, 24
         Amaryllis as Roman curia: 82
      myth of pure natural origins: 105
   rural retreat to write: 2, 5, 18
Petrarch (1304–1374)
   fate of Italian and Latin works differs: 4
   ideal model transgressed by Casa: 1, 84
   ideals echoed
      literary humanism: 1
      love: 8
      rural retreat: 2
   poetry-book:
      Catullan model mingling genres and reflecting personal crisis: 30
      Horace assimilated and surpassed: 29–30, 99
      closure
         recollecting and synthesizing themes: 109
         recursion and reemphasis: 111
         technique: 110
      coherence: 102
      cycle
         closural, cf. Muses, Thalia: 107
         odes: 21, 23
      models of Petrarch (q.v.) and Virgil (q.v.): 28
      order, determined by poet: 16, 129

ring structure
   Catullus 16, 36: 104
   CL I, II, III, V, VI: 94
   CL VII: 97
   CL IX: 101
   CL X: 104
   CL XIII: 111
Pole, Reginald Cardinal (1500–1558): 16–17, 81, 84
Priuli, Alvise (1470–1560): 9–11, 14, 17, 80, 81, 84, 92
progenies (child: cf. Catullus, Virgil): 94, 98
Propertius, *Eleg*. III.1.1 evoked: 2, 79

recusal (literary disavowal, demurral), cf. Casa, poetics: 80, 101, 102, 105
Robortello, Francisco (1516–1567), called to chair of Greek: 133
Rucellai, Annibale (?–1601): 3, 17, 29, 119
   memorized Virgil and Terence: 128

structure, cf. poetry-book

Tibullus: read in country by Farnesi: 6

uates (bard), cf. Virgil, Horace: 100, 103

Vergerio, Pietro Paolo (1498–1565): 86
Vettori, Pier (1499–1585): 4, 18, 20–24, 29, 33, 109–12, 114, 119, 130–36, 137–38, 140–47
Virgil
   Aeneid ordered burned, cf. Casa,

will to burn works: 3
7.41 *uatem* (bard): 100
11.508 *decus Italiae uirgo* (maid Italy's pride): 95
12.168 *magnae spes altera Romae* (great Rome's other hope): 6
appropriations from
  Golden Age: 91
  Hesperia as Promised Western Land: 91, 100, 107
  honorably defeated heroes forerunners of Italians: 108
  melancholy: 107
  vatic poetics: 100
Bucolics
  as model poetry-book (q.v.): 28
  memorized by Casa's nephew: 128
  1.5 *Amaryllis*: 82
  1.6 *otia* (leisure): 93
  1.54 Hyblaean bees: 82
  1.59–63 (figure of impossibility, *adynaton*): 111
  2.45 *huc ades* (come hither): 82
  3.111 *sat prata biberunt* (enough have meadows drunk): 111
  4.6 *redeunt Saturnia regna* (Saturn's realm returns): 91, 99
  4.7 *progenies* (q.v.): 98
  4.11 *decus hoc aeui* (this pride of the age): 95
  6.2 *Thalia*: 94
Georgics
  2.464 *illusas* (embroidered): 100
  3.217 *illecebris* (lures): 8, 121
  read in country by Farnesi: 6